Spelling
Games and
Activities

GRADE
2

Writing: Tiffany Hailey
Content Editing: Kathleen Jorgensen
Lisa Vitarisi Mathews
Copy Editing: Laurie Westrich
Art Direction: Yuki Meyer
Illustration: Mary Rojas
Cover Design: Yuki Meyer
Design/Production: Paula Acojido
Yuki Meyer
Jessica Onken

EMC 8272

Congratulations on your purchase of some of the finest teaching materials in the world.

Photocopying the pages in this book is permitted for <u>single-classroom use only.</u> Making photocopies for additional classes or schools is prohibited.

For information about other Evan-Moor products, call 1-800-777-4362, fax 1-800-777-4332, or visit our website, www.evan-moor.com.

CPSIA: Sheridan Saline, Inc., Saline, MI, USA [10/2023]

Contents

What's in *Spelling Games and Activities* 4

How to Use *Spelling Games and Activities* 7

Spelling Word List 8

Themed Units

Outdoor Fun 11

Words about the outdoors that have the **-ing** ending and vowel digraph **ai**

Can You Hear It? 21

Words about sounds (onomatopoeia) featuring consonant blends **cl**, **cr**, **sn**, and **sw**; consonant digraphs **ch**, **ck**, and **sh**; and diphthong **ow**

Can You Feel It? 31

Words about how things feel featuring words with long **e** or **i** spelled **y**; **r**-controlled vowels; and consonant blends **fl**, **sl**, **sm**, **sp**, and **st**

Let's Take a Trip! 41

Words about traveling featuring consonant blends **pl** and **tr**; compound words; and vowel digraphs **ai** and **ui**

Game Night 51

Words about games featuring alternate spellings of the **short u** sound and **r**-controlled vowels

Pajama Party 61

Words about a sleepover featuring consonant blends **bl** and **sl**; **r**-controlled vowels; and compound words

Go, Go, Go! 71

Words about racing featuring consonant blends **dr**, **fl**, **sp**, and **tr**; the schwa sound; and compound words

Superheroes 81

Words about superheroes featuring consonant blends **br**, **pr**, **sk**, **sm**, and **str**; **r**-controlled vowels; and diphthong **ow**

Extra Practice Worksheets 91

Spelling Strategies 152

Answer Key 160

What's in *Spelling Games and Activities*

Support for Writing

Spelling skills are essential for children to practice in order to communicate well in writing. Many people rely on technology to fix their spelling, but technology can only guess what the writer means. Spelling must be accurate to be understood. Even though there are many spelling rules and even more exceptions, spelling practice can help students understand those rules and apply them to their writing.

Spelling Games and Activities gives you two ways to help your students practice spelling:

- the engaging themed unit section, which brings together related words in grade-appropriate contexts in fun and interesting ways

- the extra practice worksheets section, which uses words from Evan-Moor's *Building Spelling Skills* series and can be used to enrich those lessons or on its own

8 Themed Units

Spelling Games and Activities offers 8 units of grade-level topics that engage students and provide context for practicing spelling useful words. Each unit introduces 10 theme-related words along with the spelling patterns and rules that are used in those words. The unit continues with fun puzzles, cutouts, and other activities to practice writing and spelling the words, followed by a game or other special activity done as a class or in small groups.

Unit Features

You can assign all the pages in a cohesive unit or choose individual worksheets as needed to support your spelling program or to reinforce words learned in other content areas. Each 10-page unit provides a set of spelling words and related spelling tips, a variety of activity pages, and a game or project with teacher directions.

Unit Overview ··

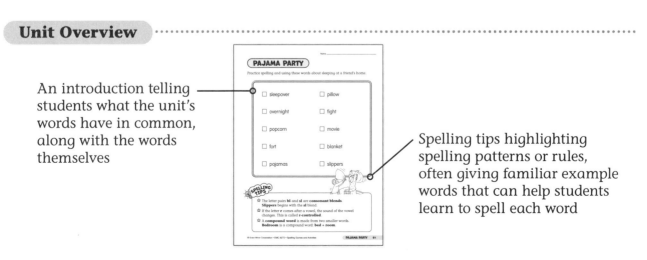

An introduction telling students what the unit's words have in common, along with the words themselves

Spelling tips highlighting spelling patterns or rules, often giving familiar example words that can help students learn to spell each word

Theme-Based Activity Pages

There are a wide variety of theme-based activities in every theme unit. These are some examples.

Finish or fix words

Students use art clues to find missing letters, unscramble words, or correct misspelled words.

Make a path

Students connect words or follow a maze using spelling patterns to reach the end.

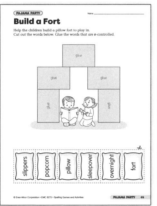

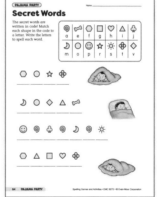

Cut and glue

Students cut and glue letters or words to categorize words or complete a picture.

Decode words and messages

Students use a fun shape code to practice writing spelling words.

Game, Activity, or Hands-on Center

A fun card game, board game, or creative activity lets students practice their words in a small or large group setting.

A page of instructions and materials for the teacher is included.

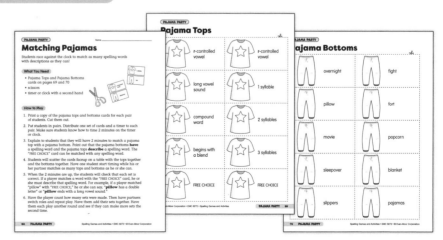

Extra Practice Worksheets

Students apply the same spelling tips from the themed units to sets of words from *Building Spelling Skills*. These pages can be used independently or with any spelling series.

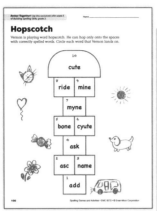
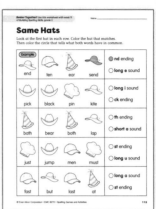
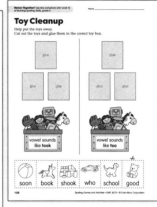

Additional Resources

Spelling Strategies

A variety of useful strategies that help students learn a word's spelling by analyzing sounds and word structures or by using dictionary skills and memory aids

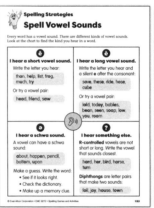
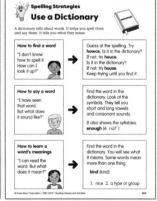

Spelling Word List

Alphabetized glossary of all spelling words in the book

Answer Key

Provided for any page that has student answers. The correct answer or a sample response is shown unless the question is completely open-ended.

How to Use *Spelling Games and Activities*

Flexible Use

Decide which pages you will use. You can use an entire unit from the themed section, pages focusing on a particular skill, or extra practice pages that apply skills to different words. Then print copies for your students. It is recommended that you include the introduction page that provides helpful spelling tips for the skills you're working on.

Connections to Other Subjects

The units in this book were chosen to represent common experiences of children in second grade, along with general grade-level words. These topics may relate to other subjects you are teaching and could augment other lessons. For example, Can You Hear It? and Superheroes could be used with a reading or language arts lesson focusing on sounds or characters in stories. The Can You Feel It? unit could extend a science lesson about characteristics and making observations. Outdoor Fun could be used when students must spend recess inside on a rainy day. Use any set of spelling words with a handwriting lesson for extra practice in both.

Extend the Challenge or the Words

If you find an activity or game particularly useful, feel free to use it as a template for other sets of spelling words or other features of the same words. For example, the activity on page 26 asks students to color leaves with words that have a short vowel. You could also ask them to color leaves with words that start with a blend or have a vowel digraph. You could also change the words on the leaves and give students a new target.

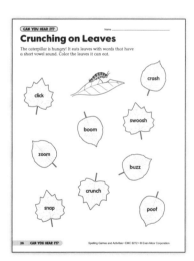

Use the Extra Practice Worksheets

If you want additional practice on specific skills or want students to practice applying skills to a new set of words, use pages from the extra practice section. This section features all the spelling words from Evan-Moor's *Building Spelling Skills* weekly lessons. If you are using *Building Spelling Skills*, you can use these extra practice worksheets to enhance your weekly lessons, giving students more practice with the same words.

Spelling Word List

about	blanket	children	father
add	blew	click	fawn
after	board	coat	fight
again	boat	come	find
ahead	boil	cook	first
airport	bone	could	fishing
along	book	crash	flag
an	boom	crunch	flew
and	both	cute	float
any	box	day	fluffy
anything	boy	dice	fly
are	brave	did	for
around	bring	didn't	fort
as	brother	directions	found
ask	brown	dive	four
at	bumpy	diving	fox
award	buzz	do	friend
away	by	doing	from
back	cake	down	fun
bank	call	draw	funny
bath	came	dress	fuzzy
be	camping	drive	game
because	can	drop	gave
bee	candle	dry	get
before	candy	each	gift
behind	cape	eat	girl
belong	card	egg	give
big	cards	end	go
birthday	chain	explore	going
black	chase	fast	good

got	just	much	pillow
green	kind	must	place
had	kite	my	play
hand	know	name	played
happy	land	nap	players
hard	last	new	poof
has	less	nice	popcorn
have	letter	no	pow
he	like	not	power
helmet	line	now	present
help	little	number	protect
her	live	of	pull
here	long	off	puppy
hero	look	oil	push
hiking	looked	old	put
him	lost	on	queen
his	love	one	quick
holiday	made	or	race
home	make	other	rain
hop	making	our	ran
hot	man	out	read
hotel	many	outside	red
house	map	over	relax
how	mask	overnight	ride
hurt	may	pack	riding
I	mean	paint	ring
if	men	pajamas	roll
in	mine	part	root
inside	mix	party	round
into	more	paw	run
it	most	people	running
jam	mother	pet	said
jumping	movie	pick	sailing

save	soon	there	was
saw	speed	these	water
say	spiky	they	way
school	stand	thing	we
score	star	this	well
seatbelt	start	ticket	went
see	stick	time	were
send	sticky	tire	wet
sent	still	to	what
she	sting	today	when
sheep	stone	told	where
shook	stop	too	which
shop	stopped	took	who
shout	store	toy	why
show	strong	track	will
side	such	train	wish
silly	suit	travel	with
sing	suitcase	treat	won
sister	sunny	tree	would
sledding	super	trick	yell
sleepover	surfing	trip	yes
slimy	swimming	try	you
slippers	swoosh	trying	your
slow	take	turn	zoo
small	team	two	zoom
smart	tell	under	
smooth	than	up	
snap	thank	us	
so	that	use	
soft	the	very	
soil	their	wait	
some	them	wall	
something	then	want	

 Spelling Games and Activities • EMC 8272 • © Evan-Moor Corporation

OUTDOOR FUN

Practice spelling and using these words about things to do outdoors.

☐ camping   ☐ sailing

☐ fishing   ☐ surfing

☐ riding   ☐ diving

☐ sledding   ☐ swimming

☐ hiking   ☐ jumping

 SPELLING TIPS

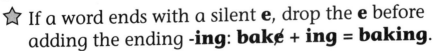

⭐ If a word ends with a silent **e**, drop the **e** before adding the ending -**ing**: **bake** + **ing** = **baking**.

⭐ When a word has one syllable and a short vowel, double the consonant before adding -**ing**: **run** + **n** + **ing** = **running**.

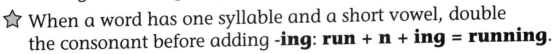

⭐ The vowel pair **ai** is a vowel digraph. It has a **long a** sound.

Name _____

Fishing for Short Sounds

Color all the fish that have a short vowel sound.

Name _____

Weekend Plans

Read the clues. Then write a word from the box to tell what each child did over the weekend.

camping   sailing   surfing   swimming

I put on a bathing suit and went in the pool.

My dad and I slept in a tent in the forest.

My grandma and I saw whales on our boat ride.

I rode big waves on my board at the beach!

Shadow Matching

Name _____

Cut out the pictures and words on page 15. Look at the shadows.
Glue the correct picture and correctly spelled word to match the shadow.

glue

glue

glue

glue

glue

glue

glue

glue

Spelling Games and Activities • EMC 8272 • © Evan-Moor Corporation

Shadow Matching, *continued*

surfing	riding	fishing
surphing	sailing	camping
fisheng	saleing	jumping

Name _____

Letter to a Friend

Help Lance write a letter to his friend Ling.
Read the sentences. Write words that end in
-ing to finish the sentences.

diving	hiking	riding	sledding	swimming

Hi Ling,

    I had a great weekend with my family.
The first day we went _____
up the mountains. Then we went horseback
_____ through the woods.
We stopped at the big lake and went
_____, too! I put on my scuba
suit and went _____ for treasure.
I found a shiny coin!

    I can't wait to go _____ with
you next weekend. I'm ready for the snow!

        Your friend,

        Lance

Spelling Games and Activities • EMC 8272 • © Evan-Moor Corporation

Name _____

Summer Break

Color the picture to see what Jameela did over summer break.

red — words with a **double letter**

green — words with a **long i** sound

yellow — words with a **short vowel** sound

blue — words with the **vowel digraph ai**

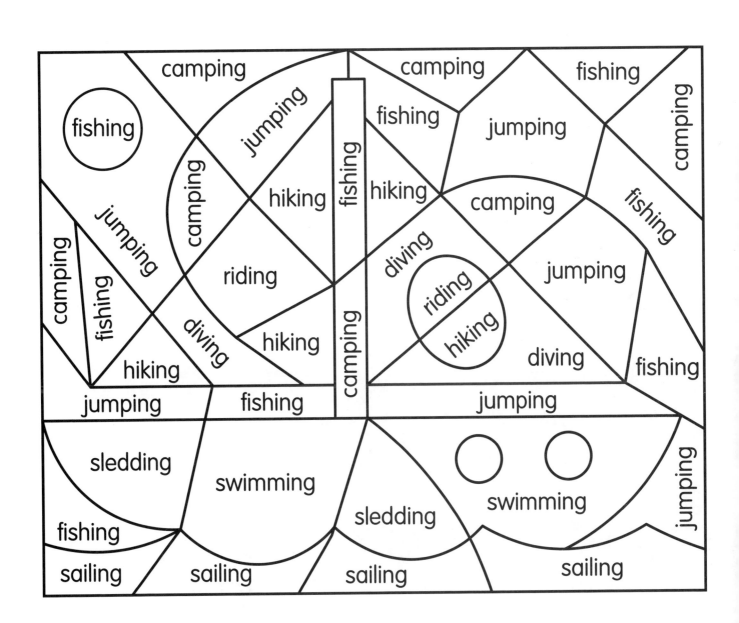

Name _____

Jump Across

Help Apollo jump across the pond. Color the rocks that have words with a long vowel sound.

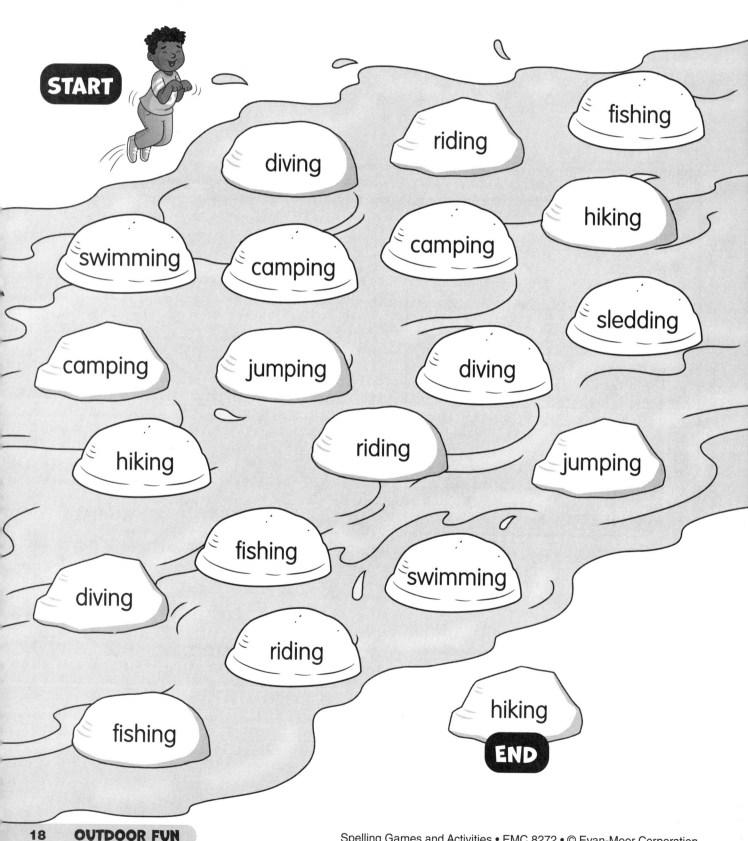

Name _____

Act It Out!

Students act out spelling words.

jumping

riding

What You Need

- Act It Out Cards on page 20
- scissors
- sheet of paper
- pencil
- timer or clock with a second hand
- card stock, laminator, or contact paper (optional)

How to Play

1. Print a copy of the Act It Out Cards for each group of students. To make cards more sturdy, copy onto card stock or use a laminator or contact paper to protect paper copies. Then cut out the cards.

2. Put students in groups of 4 and distribute a set of cards to each group, along with a timer. Have them shuffle the deck of cards and place them facedown in a stack. Make sure students know how to time 1 minute on the timer or clock.

3. Have each group divide into 2 teams. Explain to students that each person will have a role on the team:

   - **Actor:** one player takes a card from the deck and silently acts out the word on the card.
   - **Guesser:** that player's teammate tries to guess the word and then spell it.
   - **Timekeeper:** one player on the opposite team uses the timer or clock.
   - **Spellchecker:** the other player on the opposite team checks answers.

   Players change roles for each new word.

4. The timekeeper gives the actor 1 minute to act out the word. When the teammate guesses correctly, he or she spells the word (out loud or on paper). If the spellchecker says the spelling is correct, the player keeps the card. The team with the most cards wins the game.

Act It Out Cards

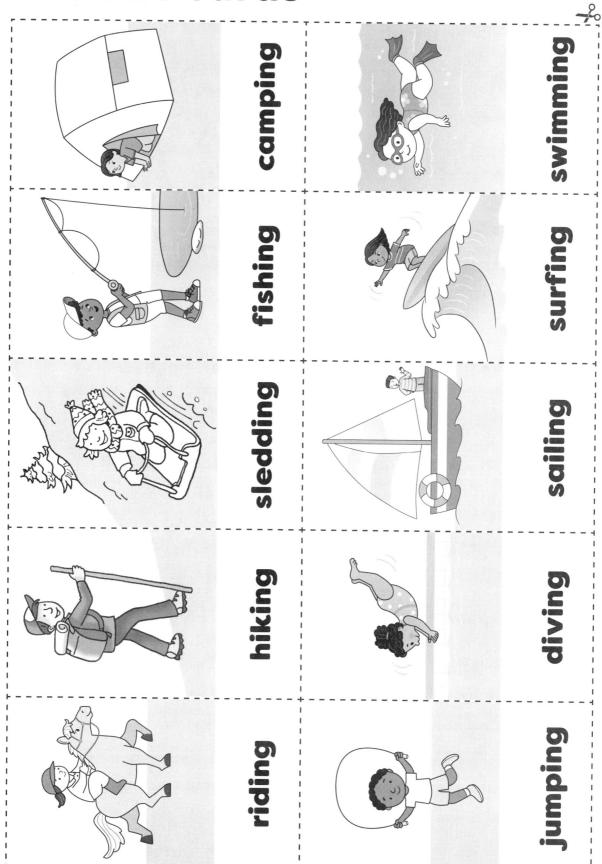

camping

swimming

fishing

surfing

sledding

sailing

hiking

diving

riding

jumping

Spelling Games and Activities • EMC 8272 • © Evan-Moor Corporation

CAN YOU HEAR IT?

Practice spelling and using these words about sounds.

☐ poof   ☐ click

☐ boom   ☐ snap

☐ zoom   ☐ crunch

☐ swoosh   ☐ crash

☐ buzz   ☐ pow

 SPELLING TIPS

⭐ The letter pairs **cl**, **cr**, **sn**, and **sw** are **consonant blends**. **Crack** begins with the **cr** blend.

⭐ The letter pairs **ch**, **ck**, and **sh** are **consonant digraphs**. **Splash** ends with the **sh** digraph.

⭐ The letter pair **ow** is a **diphthong**. It has two sounds that are said together.

Name _____

What Sound Is It?

Draw a line to show what sound each action will make.

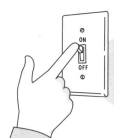 turning on a light switch

 fireworks going off

 a bee flying by

 a speeding car

 a magician disappearing

zoom

buzz

click

poof

boom

Spelling Games and Activities • EMC 8272 • © Evan-Moor Corporation

Two Letters, One Sound

Cut out the pictures on page 24. Glue to complete the picture and a word that ends in a digraph. Then write the word.

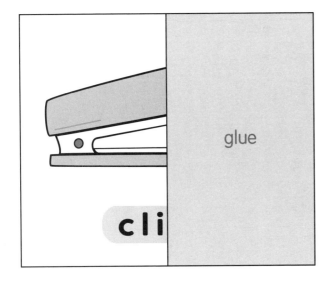

cli

_____

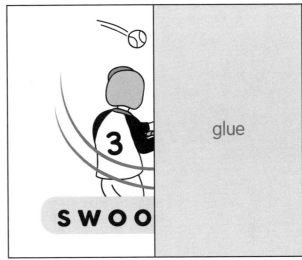

swoo

_____

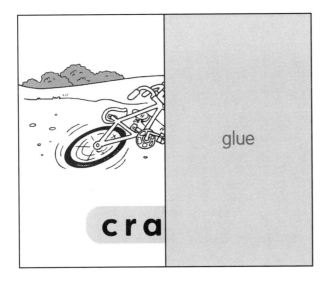

cra

_____

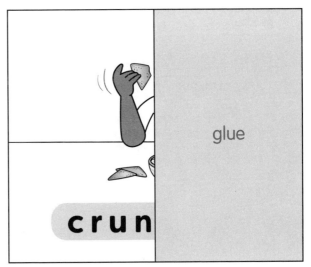

crun

_____

Two Letters, One Sound, *continued*

Spelling Games and Activities • EMC 8272 • © Evan-Moor Corporation

Name _____

Sounds on the Playground

Look at the picture.
Write a word from the box that tells
about the sound you will hear from the
children playing on the playground.

crash	crunch	pow
snap	swoosh	

_____

_____

_____

_____

Name _____

Crunching on Leaves

The caterpillar is hungry! It eats leaves with words that have a short vowel sound. Color the leaves it can eat.

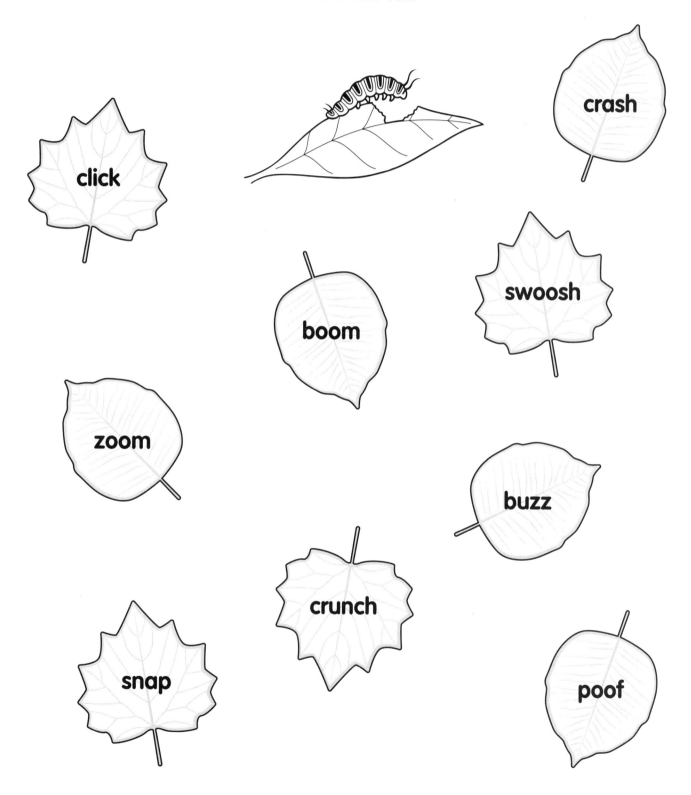

Spelling Games and Activities • EMC 8272 • © Evan-Moor Corporation

Name _____

Listen to the Speaker

What sound is playing on the speaker?
Cut out the letters. Glue them to finish
spelling words that start with a blend.
Then write the word.

| click | snap |
| crunch | swoosh |

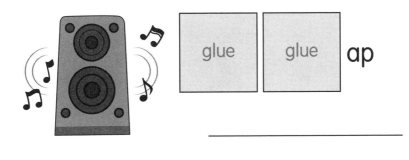

ap

_____

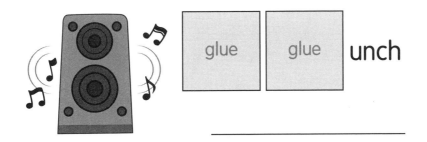

unch

_____

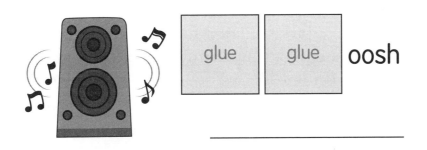

oosh

_____

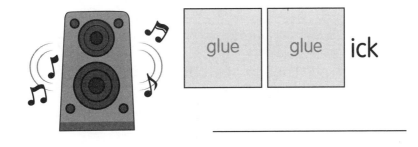

ick

_____

c

n

r

l

s

s

c

w

Name _____

Comic Strip

Students use their spelling words and creativity to make a comic strip.

What You Need

- Can You Hear It? spelling word list on page 21
- Comic Strip Example on page 29 or your own examples of comics
- Comic Strip Frame on page 30
- white paper
- pencil
- colored pencils or markers

What to Do

1. Print a copy of the Comic Strip Example and the Comic Strip Frame for each student. Print a copy of the spelling word list for every pair of students.

2. Put students in pairs. Distribute the Comic Strip Example (or your own examples) and a Comic Strip Frame to each student along with paper, pencils, and colored pencils or markers. Point out that a comic story uses word bubbles and dialogue between characters to tell what is going on. Read the comic aloud for the students. Show how "sound words" (onomatopoeia) such as their spelling words are written big to show sound in the story.

3. Explain to students that they will use their imagination and creativity to make their own comic using their spelling words.

4. Ask students to tell about any comics that they like to read. If needed, help the class brainstorm ideas for comic strip characters or scenes.

5. Have students work with their partner to sketch their own comic using at least two spelling words. When they are happy with their comic, have them draw it neatly in the Comic Strip Frame and color it. If time allows, have students read and show their comic to the class.

Name _____

Comic Strip Example

BY IGOR ŻAKOWSKI

BLACK DUCKS

Comic Strip Frame

Name _____

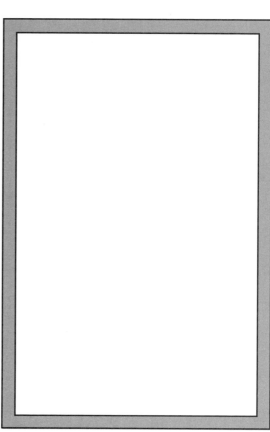
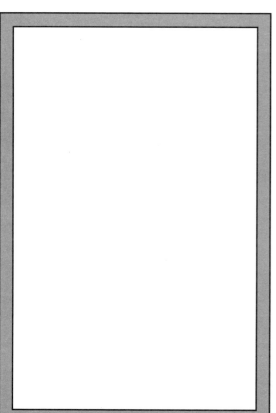

Spelling Games and Activities • EMC 8272 • © Evan-Moor Corporation

CAN YOU FEEL IT?

Practice spelling and using these words about how things feel.

☐ hard   ☐ soft

☐ wet   ☐ dry

☐ smooth   ☐ bumpy

☐ spiky   ☐ slimy

☐ fluffy   ☐ sticky

SPELLING TIPS

☆ The **letter y** is sometimes a vowel that has a **long e** or a **long i** sound. **Funny** ends with a **long e** sound. **Sky** ends with a **long i** sound.

☆ If the letter **r** comes after a vowel, the sound of the vowel changes. This is called **r-controlled**.

☆ The letter pairs **fl**, **sl**, **sm**, **sp**, and **st** are **consonant blends**. **Slippery** begins with the **sl** blend.

Name _____

Missing Pets

Write the missing letters to finish spelling each word.

○

| bumpy | fluffy | slimy | smooth | spiky |

Missing Pets

bu _____ y
frog

_____ imy
snail

○

_____ uffy
bunny

_____ iky
hedgehog

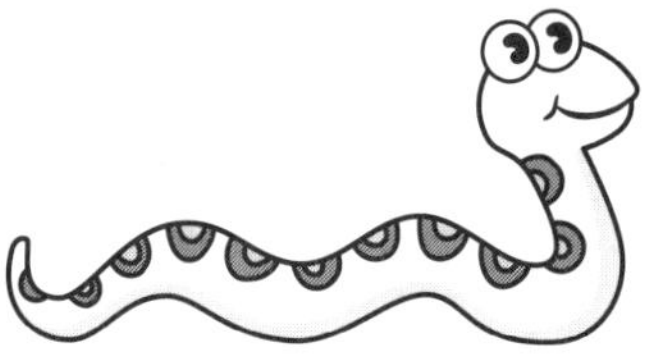

○

sm _____ th
snake

Spelling Games and Activities • EMC 8272 • © Evan-Moor Corporation

Name _____

What Do You Need?

Write a word to finish the sentence. Then draw a line to match the word and give each person what he or she needs.

 I need to stay _____ in the rain.

wet

 My plants need to get _____ to grow.

sticky

 I need a _____ pillow to sleep on.

dry

 I need something _____ to hang my picture on the wall.

soft

 I need a _____ hat to keep me safe when I ride my bike.

hard

© Evan-Moor Corporation • EMC 8272 • Spelling Games and Activities

All Aboard!

Cut out the train cars on page 35.
Glue the train cars with words that end with a **long e** sound.

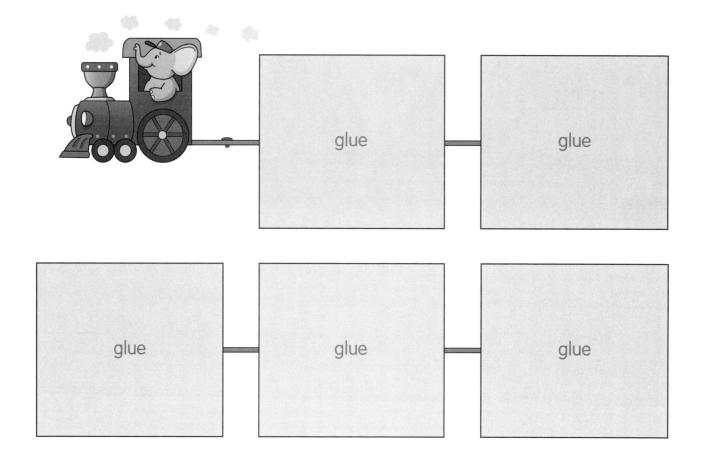

Spelling Games and Activities • EMC 8272 • © Evan-Moor Corporation

All Aboard!, *continued*

smooth

slimy

sticky

fluffy

hard

spiky

dry

bumpy

Toy Maze

Name _____

Help Zuri put her toys away in the toy box.
Follow the words that have a short vowel sound.

START

slimy

spiky

bumpy

fluffy

soft

soft

bumpy

wet

fluffy

bumpy

sticky

sticky

slimy

dry

fluffy

wet

bumpy

spiky

smooth

END

dry

TOYS

Spelling Games and Activities • EMC 8272 • © Evan-Moor Corporation

Name _____

In the Blender

Unscramble the letters in the blender to spell a word.

| dry | fluffy | slimy | smooth | spiky | sticky |

_____

_____

CAN YOU FEEL IT?

Word Art

Students use their spelling words to make creative word art.

What You Need

- Word Art Examples on page 39
- Word Art Planning on page 40
- white paper
- pencil
- crayons, colored pencils, or markers

What You Do

1. Print a copy of the Word Art Examples and Word Art Planning for every student.

2. Put students in pairs. Distribute one copy of the examples and planning sheets and two sheets of white paper to each student, along with the art supplies.

3. Explain to students that they will use their imagination and creativity to make art out of their spelling words. Have students look over the Word Art Examples to see if they can guess each word and find the letters in each picture.

4. Guide students through the Word Art Planning. Have students choose the two words at the top of the page that they would like to make into art. Then have students write or draw words or pictures that come to mind when they hear the spelling words they chose. For example, when you hear the word **fuzzy**, you might think of a stuffed animal, a sweater, or a blanket.

5. Have students work with their partner to sketch their word art on white paper. When they are happy with their design, have them decorate it with art supplies.

Spelling Games and Activities • EMC 8272 • © Evan-Moor Corporation

Name _____

Word Art Examples

Word Art Planning

1. Circle two spelling words that you would like to make into art.

bumpy	dry	hard	fluffy	slimy
smooth	soft	spiky	sticky	wet

2. Write the words you chose at the top of each box below.
   Then write or draw what you think of when you hear the word.

(Example) **fuzzy**

teddy bear   fur
dog   hairy

Spelling Games and Activities • EMC 8272 • © Evan-Moor Corporation

LET'S TAKE A TRIP!

Practice spelling and using these words about visiting different places.

☐ airport   ☐ holiday

☐ suitcase   ☐ hotel

☐ directions   ☐ ticket

☐ explore   ☐ travel

☐ relax   ☐ map

SPELLING TIPS

⭐ The letter pairs **pl** and **tr** are **consonant blends**. **Train** begins with the **tr** blend. **Airplane** has the **pl** blend in the middle.

⭐ A **compound word** is made from two smaller words. **Railroad** is a compound word: **rail** + **road**.

⭐ The vowel pairs **ai** and **ui** are vowel digraphs.

Name _____

Pack the Suitcase

Look at the word below the suitcase.
Circle the items with the letters that spell the word.

map	n	t	o	m	a	p	k
hotel	h	o	t	e	l	b	z
relax	y	r	e	l	a	x	s
travel	j	t	r	a	v	e	l

Spelling Games and Activities • EMC 8272 • © Evan-Moor Corporation

Name _____

Airplane Seats

Help the children find their seats on the airplane. Cut out the children on page 44. Glue each child in the correct part of the airplane below.

words with 3 syllables

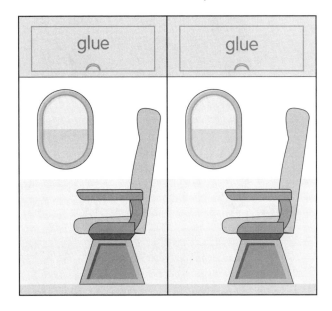

compound words

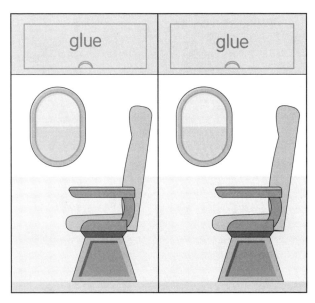

word with a **long e** sound

words with a consonant blend

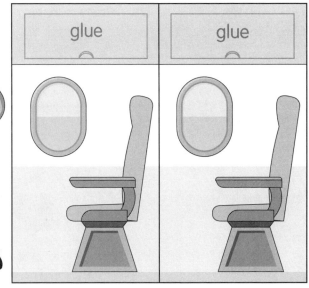

Airplane Seats, *continued*

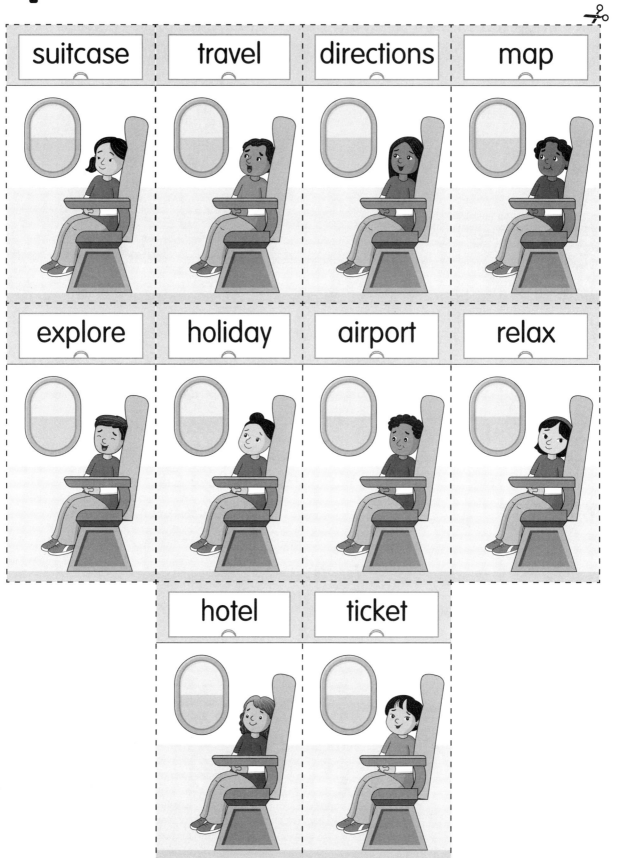

suitcase

travel

directions

map

explore

holiday

airport

relax

hotel

ticket

Name _____

Vacation Riddle

Circle the word in each pair that is not spelled correctly.
Write it correctly.

tiket, relax   __ __ __ __ __
                                  2

travel, arport   __ __ __ __ __ __
                        4

mapp, hotel   __ __ __
            1

airport, explor   __ __ __ __ __ __
                      3

direcshuns, holiday   __ __ __ __ __ __ __ __
                                          6

sutecase, explore   __ __ __ __ __ __ __ __
                               5

Now write the numbered letters in the matching spaces to answer the riddle.

Where is this plane going?

__ __ __ __ __ __
1   2   3   4   5   6

Hotel Directions

Name _____

Help the family get to the hotel.
Write the words for each step.

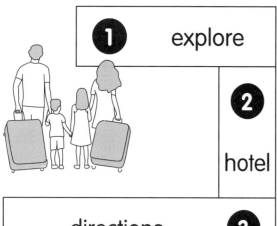

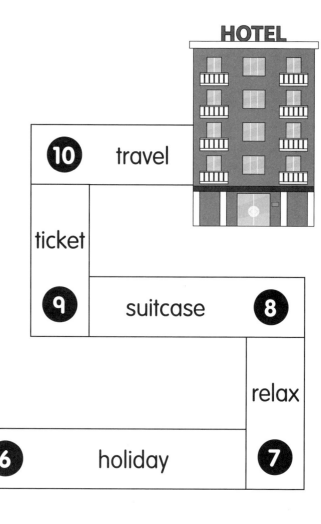

1 explore

2 hotel

10 travel

ticket

directions **3**

9 suitcase **8**

4

relax

map

5 airport

6 holiday

7

Step 1: ➡ _____

Step 2: ⬇ _____

Step 3: ⬅ _____

Step 4: ⬇ _____

Step 5: ➡ _____

Step 6: ➡ _____

Step 7: ⬆ _____

Step 8: ⬅ _____

Step 9: ⬆ _____

Step 10: ➡ _____

Spelling Games and Activities • EMC 8272 • © Evan-Moor Corporation

Travel Patterns

Draw what comes next in the pattern.
Then write the word that tells about what you drew.

airport   ticket   hotel   relax   holiday

_____

_____

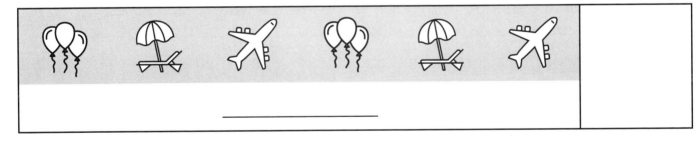

_____

_____

Travel Clues

Name _____

Students listen to clues to guess a word and spell it.

What You Need

- Teacher Clue Cards on page 49, cut out
- Word Cards on page 50, cut out

How to Play

1. Print copies of the word cards, enough to give each student in the class at least 3 cards, and cut them out. Distribute the cards to the students.

2. Cut out the Teacher Clue Cards and shuffle them into a stack.

3. Explain to students that you will read clues about a word. Students will look at their word cards to see if they have the word that fits the clue. If a student has the word, he or she shouts, "I have it!"

4. Start by reading Clue 1. If no one guesses the word correctly, read Clue 2. When someone shouts, "I have it!" ask what the word is. If correct, have the student place the card facedown and spell the word out loud.

   - If the spelling is correct, the teacher says, "You spelled it!"

   - If the spelling is incorrect, let the student know. Then say the word and invite another student to spell it.

   Give all students who have the same card and shout "I have it!" an opportunity to spell the word.

5. Continue with the clue for the next word, giving each student who shouts "I have it!" an opportunity to spell the word that matches the clue. The game ends when all Teacher Clue Cards are used.

Spelling Games and Activities • EMC 8272 • © Evan-Moor Corporation

Teacher Clue Cards

Clue 1 I begin with a **vowel digraph**, and I am a **compound word**.

Clue 2 You go here when you need to fly somewhere.

Word airport

Clue 1 I start with a **d**, and you hear **shun** near my end.

Clue 2 You tell people these so they know where to go.

Word directions

Clue 1 I have a **consonant blend** in my middle and a silent **e** at my end.

Clue 2 You do this when visiting a new place.

Word explore

Clue 1 I end with a **y**, but you hear a **long a** sound at my end.

Clue 2 This is a special day that people celebrate.

Word holiday

Clue 1 I have a **long o** sound, and I end with an **l**.

Clue 2 This is a place where you stay and sleep when you travel.

Word hotel

Clue 1 I have one syllable and a **short a** sound.

Clue 2 You can look at me to find your way.

Word map

Clue 1 I have a **long e** sound, and I end like the word **fox**.

Clue 2 I am another word for **rest**.

Word relax

Clue 1 I am a compound word that ends with a silent **e**.

Clue 2 You pack things you need in me.

Word suitcase

Clue 1 I start and end with the same letter.

Clue 2 You cannot ride on a train or airplane without me.

Word ticket

Clue 1 I begin with a **consonant blend**.

Clue 2 You do this when you go from one place to another.

Word travel

Word Cards

 airport

 directions

 explore

 holiday

 **hotel**

 **map**

 **relax**

 suitcase

 **ticket**

 **travel**

Spelling Games and Activities • EMC 8272 • © Evan-Moor Corporation

GAME NIGHT

Practice spelling and using these words about playing games.

☐ dice   ☐ roll

☐ team   ☐ players

☐ won   ☐ board

☐ lost   ☐ award

☐ cards   ☐ score

SPELLING TIPS

⭐ Sometimes other vowels make the **short u** sound.
The **o** in **one** and the **a** in **alike** have a **short u** sound.

⭐ If the letter **r** comes after a vowel, the sound of the vowel
changes. This is called **r-controlled**.

Name _____

Guess What?

Read the clue. Write a spelling word.
Then cut out the game pieces on page 53.
Use the chart below to match each child's spelling word with
a game piece. Then glue the game piece next to the word.

♜ award	🐴 board	♟ dice	👞 lost
🐕 players	🚗 roll	🎩 team	🛥 won

 This word ends with two of the same letter.

_____

glue

 These are people who are playing a game.

_____

glue

 This is a group of people who work together.

_____

glue

 You did this when you did not win.

_____

glue

Spelling Games and Activities • EMC 8272 • © Evan-Moor Corporation

Name _____

Guess What?, *continued*

 You did this when you did not lose.

_____

glue

 This word begins with a **short u** sound.

_____

glue

 This word has a **long i** sound.

_____

glue

 This is a flat piece of wood.

_____

glue

Name _____

Game Night Teams

Help put the spelling words into teams of two. Look at the team names. Put each spelling word into the correct team. Use each word only one time.

cards	roll	score	dice
award	won	team	lost

Team
short u sound

_____ award _____

_____

Team
long i sound

_____ mice _____

_____

Team
r-controlled

_____

_____

Team
short o sound

_____ toss _____

_____

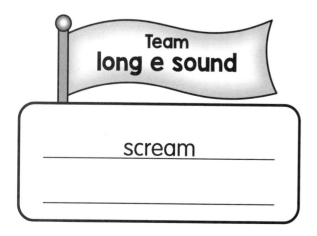

Team
long e sound

_____ scream _____

_____

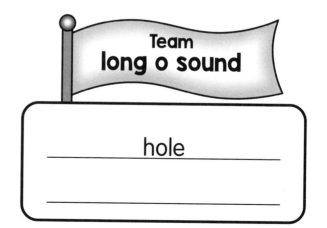

Team
long o sound

_____ hole _____

_____

Spelling Games and Activities • EMC 8272 • © Evan-Moor Corporation

GAME NIGHT

The Price Is Right

How much does each game word cost? Look at the word in the box.
Write each letter in the word and its price. Add the prices together.
Write the total price of the word.

a = $1	c = $2	d = $3	e = $4	i = $5	l = $6
m = $7	n = $8	o = $9	r = $10	t = $12	w = $13

Example

roll	team	won	dice

roll

r	$ 10
o	$ 9
l	$ 6
l	+ $ 6

$31

team

___ $___
___ $___
___ $___
___ + $___

won

___ $___
___ $___
___ $___

dice

___ $___
___ $___
___ $___
___ + $___

Name _____

Let's Play Tag!

Tag, you're it!
Read each word on the path. Follow the words that are **r-controlled**.
Tag a friend at the end of your path. Circle the friend you tagged.

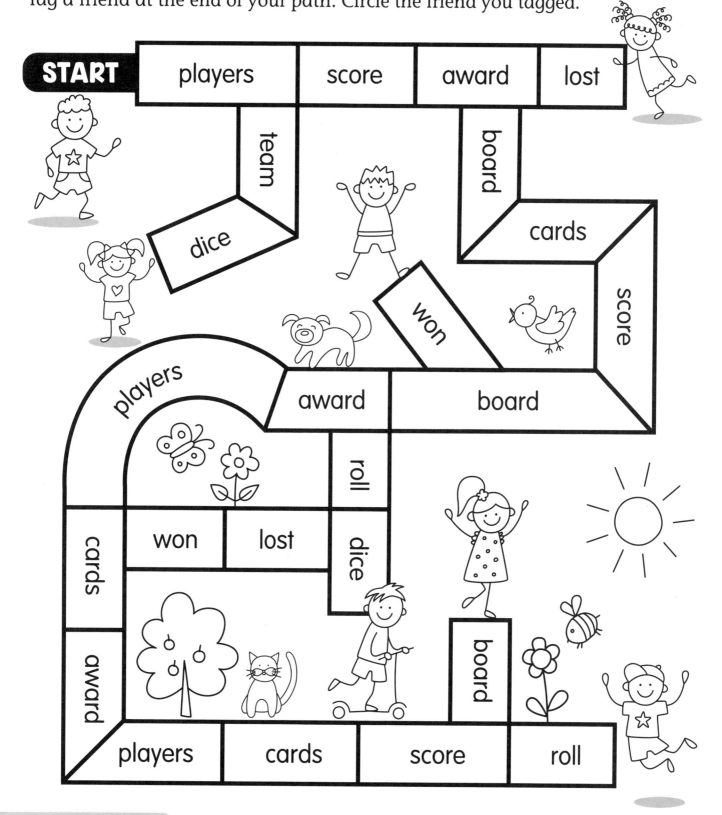

Spelling Games and Activities • EMC 8272 • © Evan-Moor Corporation

Name _____

Hide and Seek

Find the hidden letters in each picture.
Use the letters to spell an **r**-controlled word.
Write it on the lines.

award	board	cards
dice	players	score

_____ _____ _____ _____ _____

_____ _____ _____ _____ _____

_____ _____ _____ _____ _____ _____ _____

_____ _____ _____ _____ _____

Name _____

Spell It to Win It!

Students spell words to move along a game board to the finish line.

What You Need

- Game Night spelling word list on page 51
- Game Die and Game Pieces on page 59
- Game Board on page 60
- scissors
- glue or tape

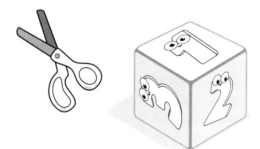

How to Play

1. Print a copy of the spelling word list and the die and game pieces for every pair of students.

2. Cut out the die and game pieces. Assemble the die and glue or tape down the tabs. Fold the bottom of the dog and cat game pieces to make them stand up.

3. Put students in pairs.

4. Distribute one die, 2 game pieces, and one game board to each pair. Have students put their game pieces on Start.

5. Explain to students that they will take turns rolling the die and moving their game piece the same number of squares. Students will then read what it says on the space, find a word from the spelling word list that follows the spelling pattern on the space, and spell the word.

6. The first person to reach the End space wins.

Spelling Games and Activities • EMC 8272 • © Evan-Moor Corporation

Game Die and Game Pieces

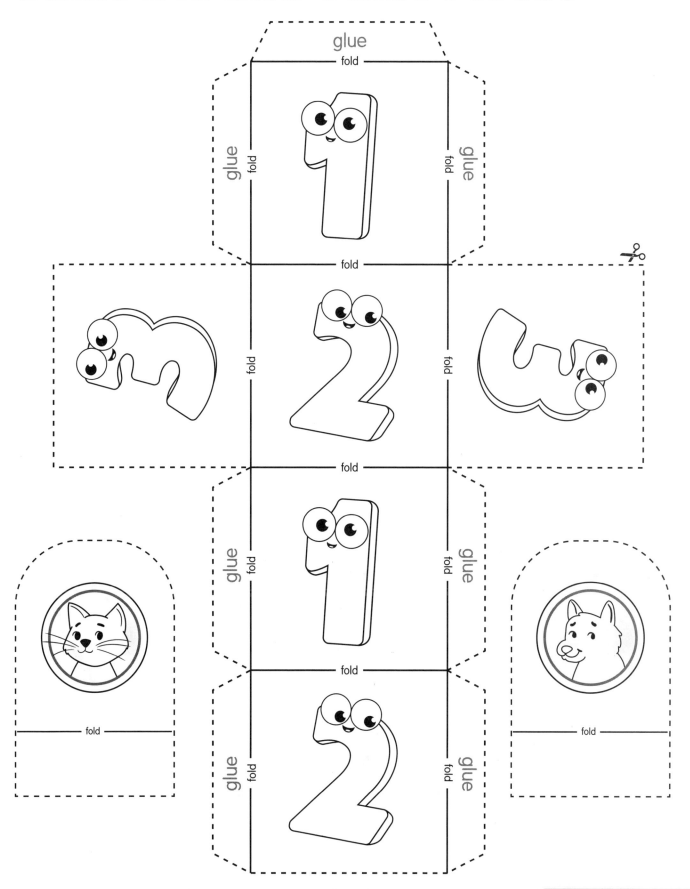

Game Board

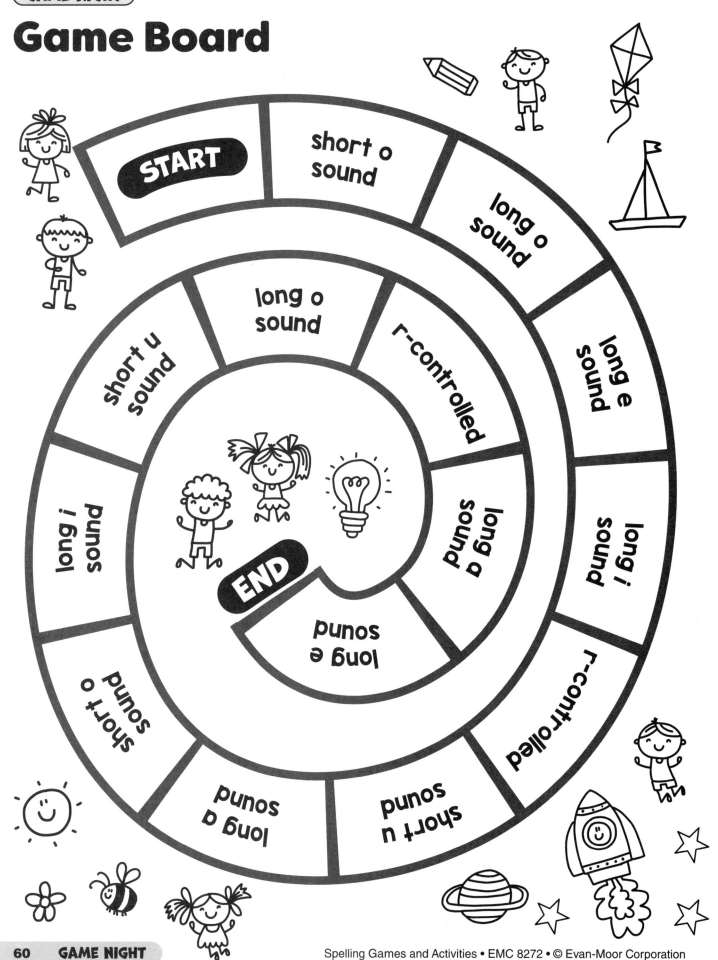

START

short o sound

long o sound

long e sound

long o sound

r-controlled

short u sound

long i sound

long a sound

long i sound

long e sound

r-controlled

short o sound

long a sound

short u sound

END

Spelling Games and Activities • EMC 8272 • © Evan-Moor Corporation

PAJAMA PARTY

Practice spelling and using these words about sleeping at a friend's home.

☐ sleepover   ☐ pillow

☐ overnight   ☐ fight

☐ popcorn   ☐ movie

☐ fort   ☐ blanket

☐ pajamas   ☐ slippers

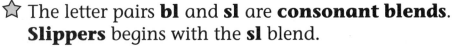

SPELLING TIPS

☆ The letter pairs **bl** and **sl** are **consonant blends**. **Slippers** begins with the **sl** blend.

☆ If the letter **r** comes after a vowel, the sound of the vowel changes. This is called **r-controlled**.

☆ A **compound word** is made from two smaller words. **Bedroom** is a compound word: **bed + room**.

Name _____

Slipper Pairs

Cut out the slippers. Glue a slipper in each row to make a compound word. Then write the word.

pop + glue =

_____

sleep +  glue =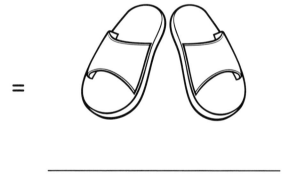

_____

over +  glue =

_____

night

corn

slippers

over

Spelling Games and Activities • EMC 8272 • © Evan-Moor Corporation

Pillow Fight

The children are having a pillow fight!
Read the word on each pillow. If the word
has a **long e** sound or a **long i** sound,
the child will win. Draw an **X** on each
child who wins.

Name _____

movie

blanket

pillow

fight

overnight

sleepover

Secret Words

The secret words are written in code! Match each shape in the code to a letter. Write the letters to spell each word.

Symbol	Letter	Symbol	Letter
spiral	a	moon	m
bone	e	circle	o
hexagon	f	smiley	p
square	g	star	r
heart	h	sun	s
triangle	i	flower	t
club	j	diamond	v

_____ _____ _____ _____

_____ _____ _____ _____ _____

_____ _____ _____ _____ _____ _____ _____

_____ _____ _____ _____ _____

Spelling Games and Activities • EMC 8272 • © Evan-Moor Corporation

Name _____

Build a Fort

Help the children build a pillow fort to play in.
Cut out the words below. Glue the words that are **r**-controlled.

Name _____

Movie Night

Help Emily reach her friends to watch a movie.
Color the squares that have words with a long vowel sound.

START	pillow	overnight	movie	fort
blanket	pajamas	fort	fight	sleepover
pillow	movie	sleepover	slippers	pillow
overnight	popcorn	fight	movie	overnight
movie	slippers	pajamas	blanket	popcorn
fight	sleepover	pillow	overnight	END

Spelling Games and Activities • EMC 8272 • © Evan-Moor Corporation

Name _____

Popped Letters

Write the missing letters to finish spelling each word.
Cross off each letter in the popcorn after you use it.

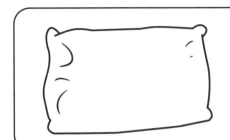

pill_____

 l

 i

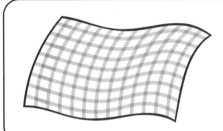

b____anket

 o

 a

popc____rn

 e

 o

mov_____

 w

a

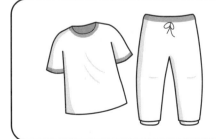

p____jam____s

Name _____

Matching Pajamas

Students race against the clock to match as many spelling words with descriptions as they can!

What You Need

- Pajama Tops and Pajama Bottoms cards on pages 69 and 70
- scissors
- timer or clock with a second hand

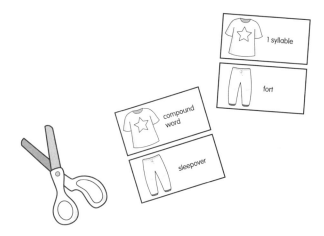

How to Play

1. Print a copy of the pajama tops and bottoms cards for each pair of students. Cut them out.

2. Put students in pairs. Distribute one set of cards and a timer to each pair. Make sure students know how to time 2 minutes on the timer or clock.

3. Explain to students that they will have 2 minutes to match a pajama top with a pajama bottom. Point out that the pajama bottoms **have** a spelling word and the pajama tops **describe** a spelling word. The "FREE CHOICE" card can be matched with any spelling word.

4. Students will scatter the cards faceup on a table with the tops together and the bottoms together. Have one student start timing while his or her partner matches as many tops and bottoms as he or she can.

5. When the 2 minutes are up, the students will check that each set is correct. If a player matches a word with the "FREE CHOICE" card, he or she must describe that spelling word. For example, if a player matched "pillow" with "FREE CHOICE," he or she can say, "**pillow** has a double letter" or "**pillow** ends with a long vowel sound."

6. Have the player count how many sets were made. Then have partners switch roles and repeat play. Have them add their sets together. Have them each play another round and see if they can make more sets the second time.

Spelling Games and Activities • EMC 8272 • © Evan-Moor Corporation

Pajama Tops

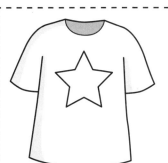 **r**-controlled vowel

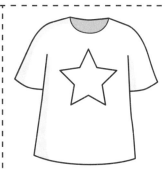 **r**-controlled vowel

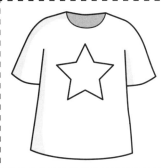 long vowel sound

 1 syllable

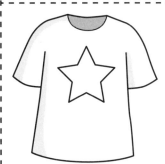 compound word

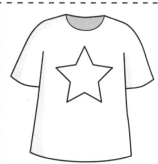 2 syllables

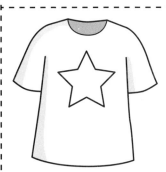 begins with a blend

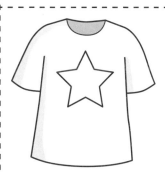 3 syllables

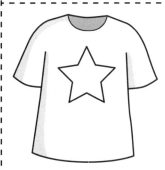 FREE CHOICE

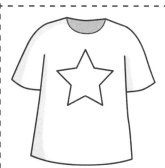 FREE CHOICE

Pajama Bottoms

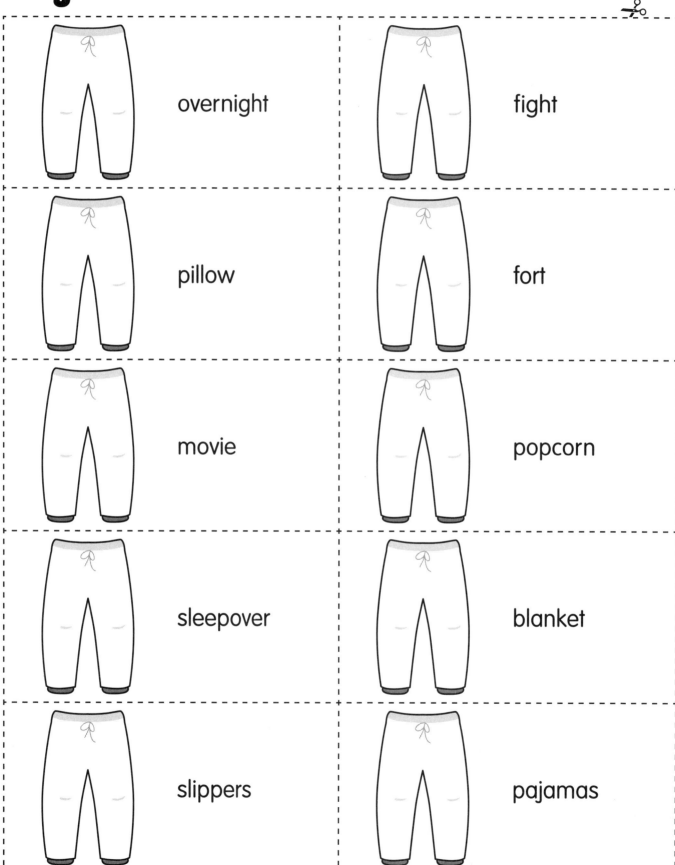

overnight

fight

pillow

fort

movie

popcorn

sleepover

blanket

slippers

pajamas

Spelling Games and Activities • EMC 8272 • © Evan-Moor Corporation

GO, GO, GO!

Practice spelling and using these words about racing.

- ☐ race
- ☐ tire
- ☐ speed
- ☐ ahead
- ☐ seatbelt

- ☐ behind
- ☐ drive
- ☐ track
- ☐ flag
- ☐ helmet

SPELLING TIPS

⭐ The letter pairs **dr**, **fl**, **sp**, and **tr** are **consonant blends**. **Truck** begins with the **tr** blend.

⭐ A **schwa** is a sound a vowel can have. Sometimes a schwa sounds like a **short u**. **Away** begins with a schwa sound. You say this word as **uh-WAY**.

⭐ A **compound word** is made from two smaller words. **Seatbelt** is a compound word: **seat + belt**.

Name _____

Pit Stop

Help the pit crew put new tires on the cars. Cut out the tires below.
Glue the tires onto the correct car.

begins with a blend

glue   glue

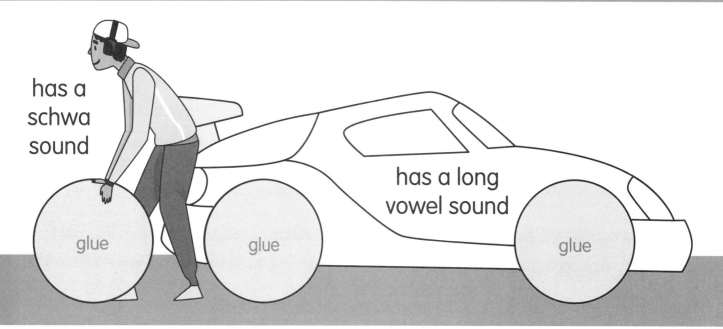

has a schwa sound

has a long vowel sound

glue   glue   glue

track   tire   ahead   race   flag

Spelling Games and Activities • EMC 8272 • © Evan-Moor Corporation

Name _____

Problem on the Track

Oh no! The cars can't move along the track because the words are misspelled. Help the cars move by spelling each word correctly.

| ahead | behind | drive | helmet | race | speed |

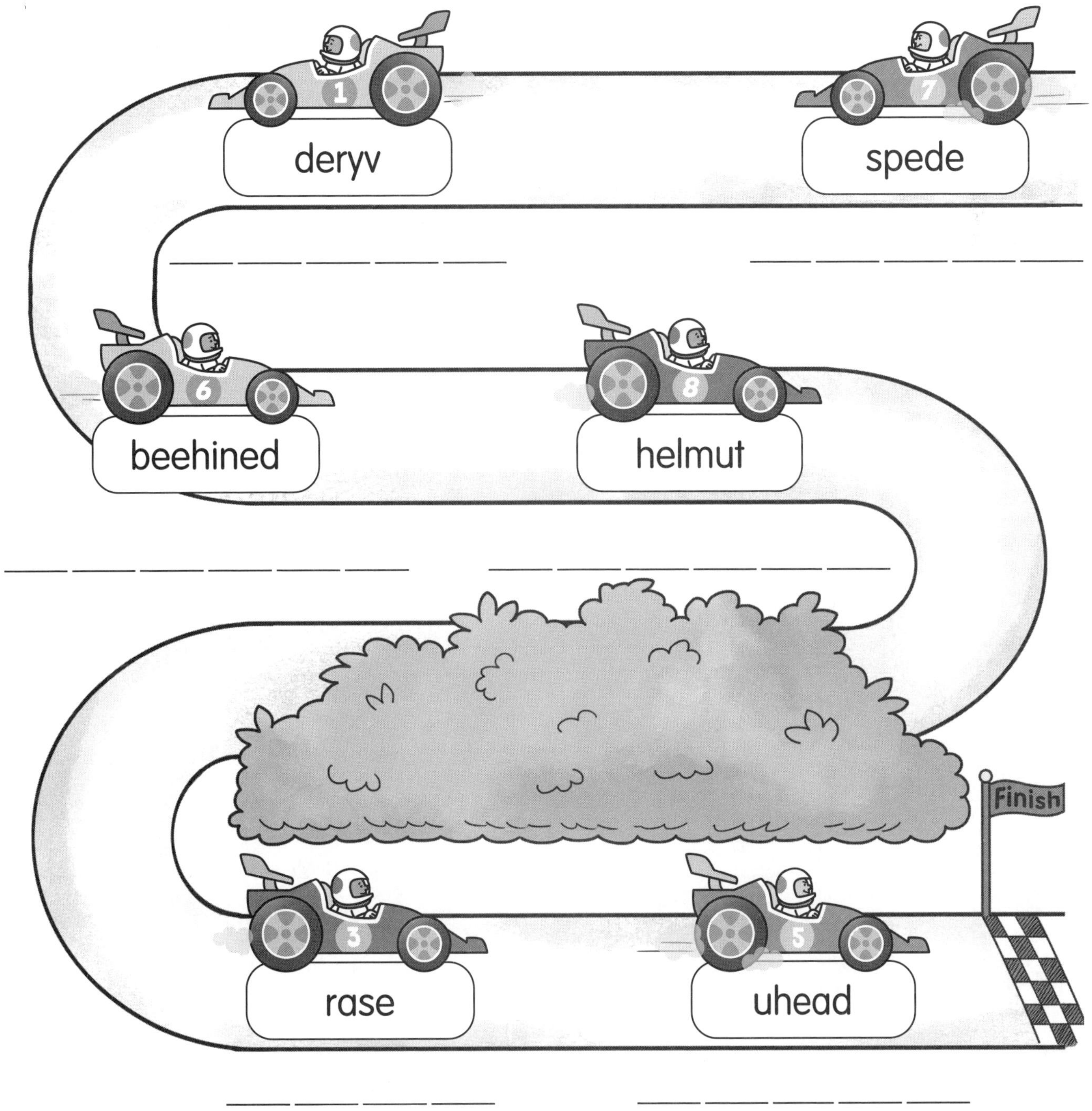

deryv _____

spede _____

beehined _____

helmut _____

rase _____

uhead _____

Finish

_____   _____

Name _____

Car Parts

Help build a car. Cut out the pictures on page 75. Glue them to make a car and spell a word.

car #1

glue	glue

car #2

glue	glue

car #3

glue	glue

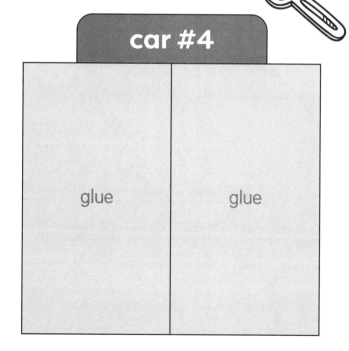

car #4

glue	glue

Spelling Games and Activities • EMC 8272 • © Evan-Moor Corporation

Car Parts, *continued*

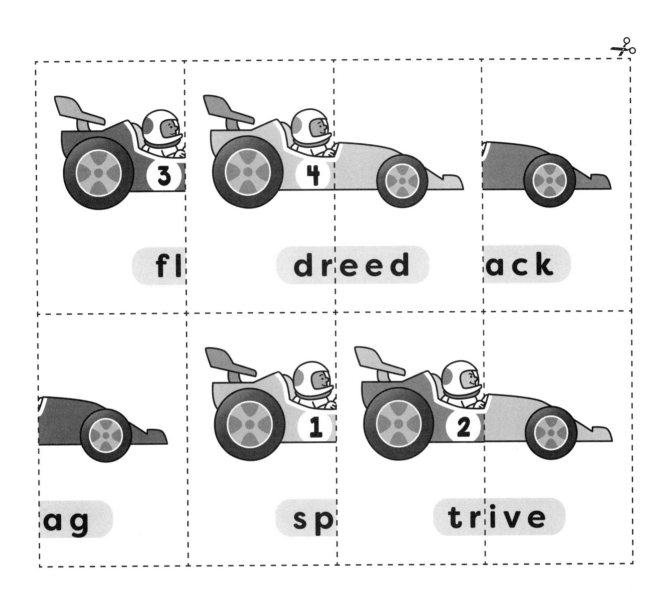

fl

dreed

ack

ag

sp

trive

Name _____

Whose Car?

Each child is cheering for a car. Read each clue. Write a word.
Then draw a line to match the child to the car that has the same word.

I have a schwa sound. _____

seatbelt

I have a **long e** sound and a double letter. _____

behind

I am a compound word. _____

ahead

I have a **long e** sound and a **long i** sound. _____

speed

Spelling Games and Activities • EMC 8272 • © Evan-Moor Corporation

Around the Track

Help the race car reach the flags at the end.
Follow the words that have a long vowel sound.

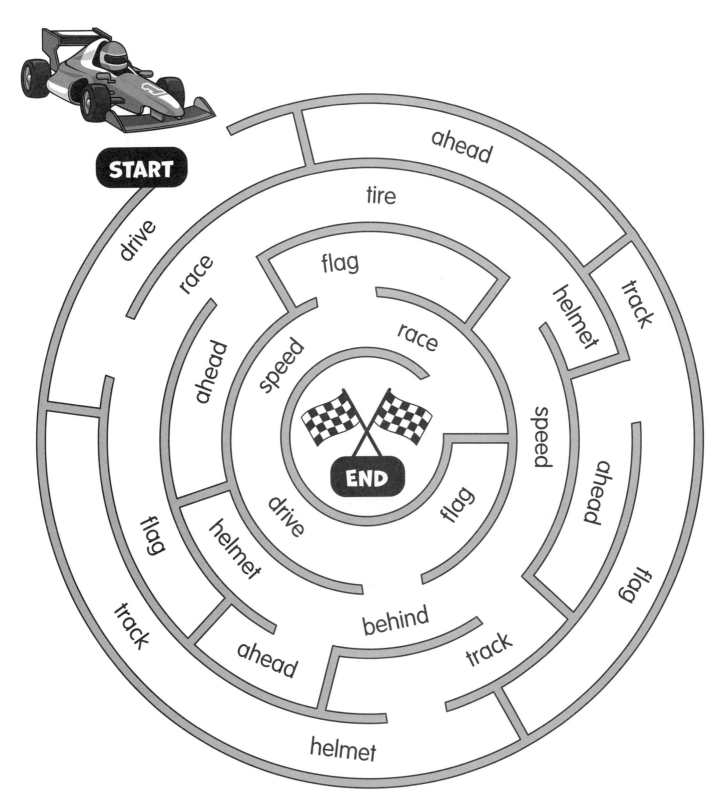

START

ahead

tire

drive

race

flag

helmet

track

speed

race

ahead

speed

END

drive

flag

ahead

helmet

flag

track

ahead

flag

behind

track

ahead

helmet

Name _____

Spelling Race

Students race against a partner to spell words and reach the finish line first.

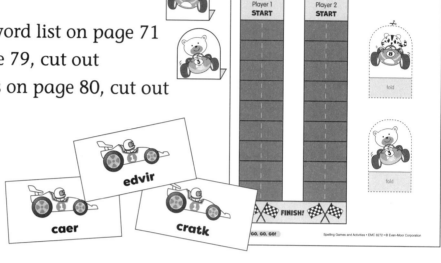

What You Need

- GO, GO, GO! spelling word list on page 71
- Race Car Cards on page 79, cut out
- Game Board and Pieces on page 80, cut out
- sheets of paper
- pencil

How to Play

1. Print a copy of the spelling word list and the Race Car Cards for every student. Print a copy of the Game Board and Pieces for every pair of students. Cut out the cards and the Game Board and Pieces.

2. Put students in pairs. Distribute 2 sets of cards, 2 game pieces, one game board, and 2 sheets of paper to each pair. Have each student shuffle their own deck of cards and place them facedown in a stack.

3. Explain to students that they will race their partner to spell words correctly and get to the finish line. When the teacher says, "Ready, set, go!" players will turn over their first card. They unscramble the letters on the card and write the correct spelling word on a sheet of paper. After a player has written the word, he or she can move his or her race car down one space on the track. The players continue to take cards, write the correct spelling words, and move their race car until it reaches Finish.

4. After both players have reached the finish line, they check the spelling of each other's list of words. If the player who reached Finish first has all 10 words spelled correctly, that player wins. If the player does not have all the words spelled correctly, the player with the most correctly spelled words wins.

Race Car Cards

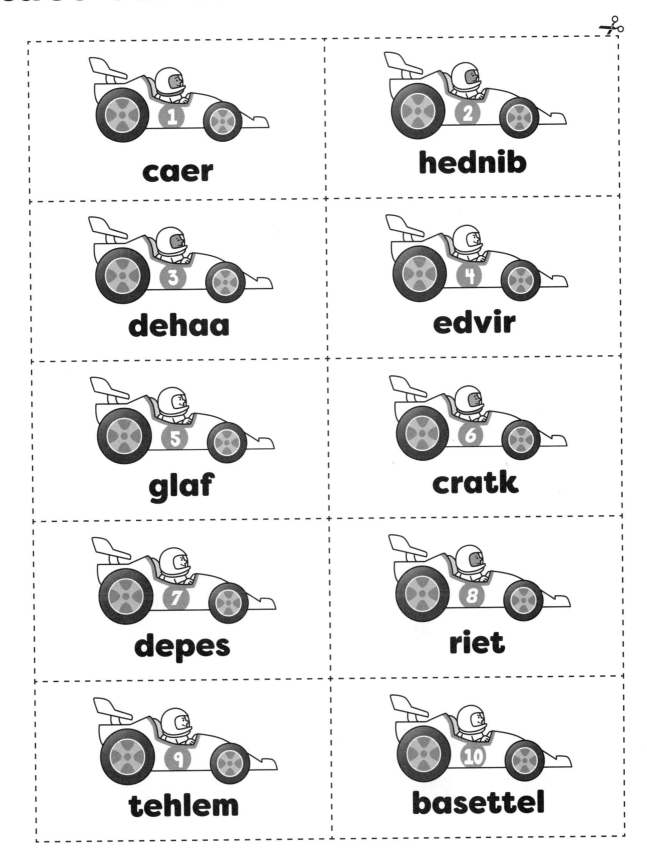

1. caer

2. hednib

3. dehaa

4. edvir

5. glaf

6. cratk

7. depes

8. riet

9. tehlem

10. basettel

Game Board and Pieces

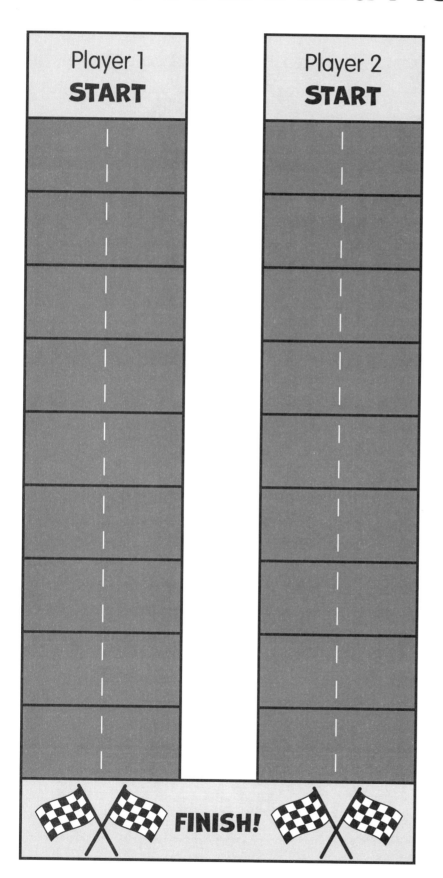

Player 1
START

Player 2
START

FINISH!

fold

fold

SUPERHEROES

Practice spelling and using these words about superheroes.

☐ super   ☐ mask

☐ hero   ☐ brave

☐ power   ☐ smart

☐ cape   ☐ strong

☐ suit   ☐ protect

SPELLING TIPS

☆ The letter groups **br**, **pr**, **sk**, **sm**, and **str** are **consonant blends**. **Stop** begins with the **st** blend. **Risk** ends with the **sk** blend.

☆ If the letter **r** comes after a vowel, the sound of the vowel changes. This is called **r-controlled**.

☆ The letter pair **ow** is a diphthong. It has two sounds that are said together.

Name _____

Smashed Windows

Oh no! A monster smashed the windows! Help the
superhero put in new windows. Cut out the letters.
Glue them to finish spelling words that have a blend.

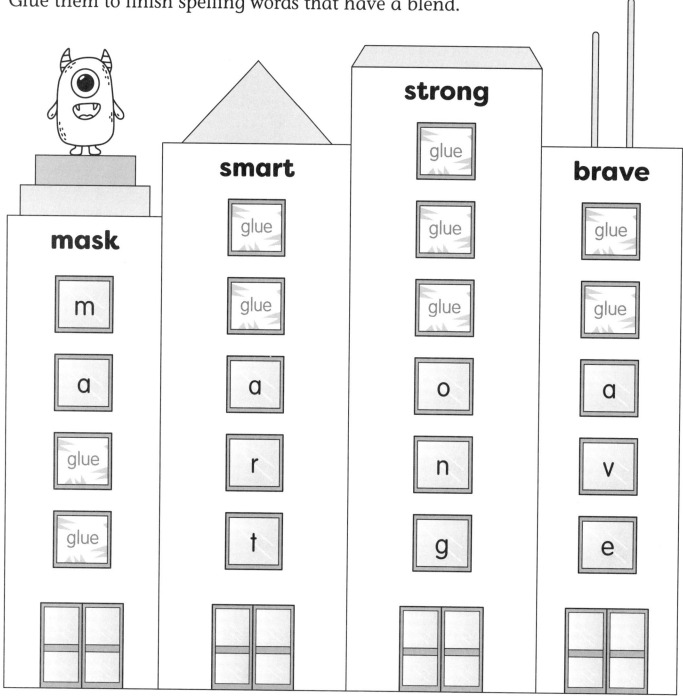

Spelling Games and Activities • EMC 8272 • © Evan-Moor Corporation

Name _____

Cookie Jar Hero

Look at the word. It is not spelled correctly.
Write it correctly.

protekt ___ ___ ___ ___ ___ ___ ___
                                    1

powur ___ ___ ___ ___ ___
                        2

cayp ___ ___ ___ ___
      4   3

| cape |
| hero |
| power |
| protect |
| suit |

soot ___ ___ ___ ___
              5

hiro ___ ___ ___ ___
          6

Now write the numbered letters in the matching spaces
to find the Cookie Jar Hero.

Who kept the cookies safe? ___ ___ ___ ___ ___ ___
                            1   2   3   4   5   6

Cathie

Stewie

Tracie

Name _____

Lost Balloons

Help! The children's balloons are flying away!
Color the balloons that match the words below the children.

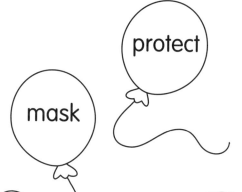

pow

cape

protect

mask

suit

mash

cap

project

power

soup

suit

cape

mask

power

protect

Spelling Games and Activities • EMC 8272 • © Evan-Moor Corporation

Name _____

Hidden Treasure

Help the hero find the hidden treasure. Cut out the puzzle pieces on page 86. Look at the clues in each box below. Then glue the puzzle piece that matches the clue. You will find the treasure!

starts with **s** and ends with **er** glue	means "a person who helps others" glue
has a vowel pair glue	starts with **p** and ends with **er** glue
starts with the blend **sm** glue	starts with the blend **br** glue
means "to keep something from being hurt" glue	starts with a blend that has 3 letters glue
has a **long a** sound glue	ends with the blend **sk** glue

Hidden Treasure, *continued*

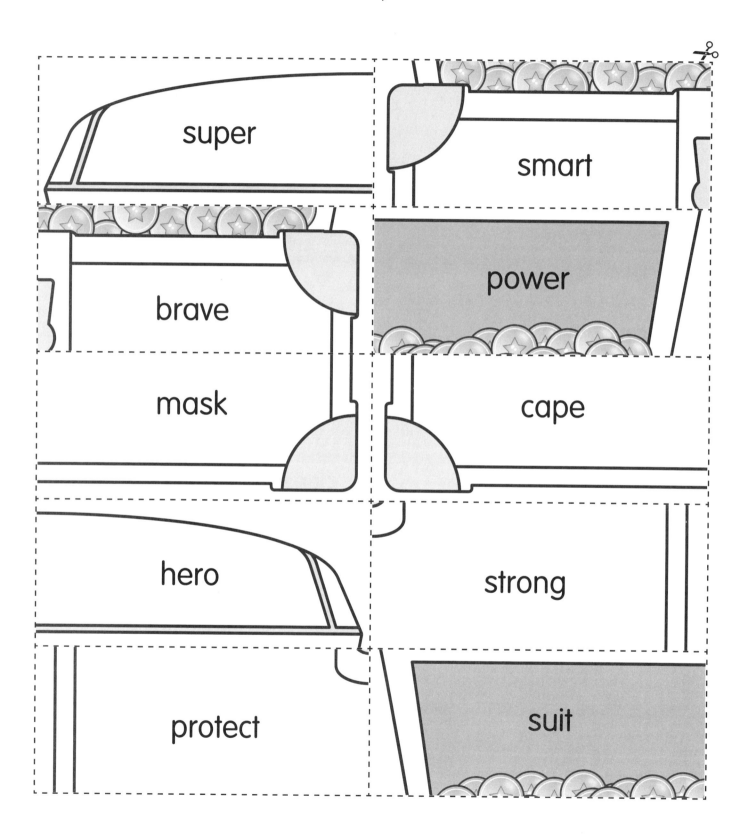

super

smart

brave

power

mask

cape

hero

strong

protect

suit

Name _____

To the Rescue

Students spell words to move along a game board and find the missing superhero.

What You Need

- Spinner and Game Pieces on page 88
- Superhero Cards on page 89
- Game Board on page 90
- card stock, laminator, or contact paper (optional)

- paper clip
- pencil
- 2 sheets of paper

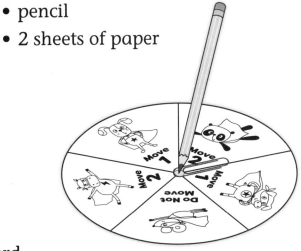

How to Play

1. Print a copy of the Spinner and Game Pieces page and the Game Board for each pair of students. Print a copy of the Superhero Cards for every student. To make cards more sturdy, copy onto card stock, or use a laminator or contact paper to protect paper copies. Then cut out the cards, spinner, and game pieces.

2. Show students how to use the spinner. Push a pencil through the end of the paper clip and into the center point of the spinner. Flick the paper clip.

3. Put students in pairs. Distribute one spinner, 2 game pieces, 2 sets of cards, and one Game Board to each pair, along with a paper clip and a pencil. Have students shuffle the cards and put them facedown in a stack. Have them put their game pieces on Start.

4. Explain to students that they will spell words to move along the board and reach the superhero. Player 1 takes a card and reads the word out loud. Player 2 writes the word on a sheet of paper. Player 1 checks the spelling. If the word is spelled correctly, Player 2 spins the paper clip and moves as shown. If the word is incorrect, Player 2 moves back 1 space.

5. Change roles for the next player's turn. Continue until the first player reaches the End space, finds the superhero, and wins the game.

Spinner and Game Pieces

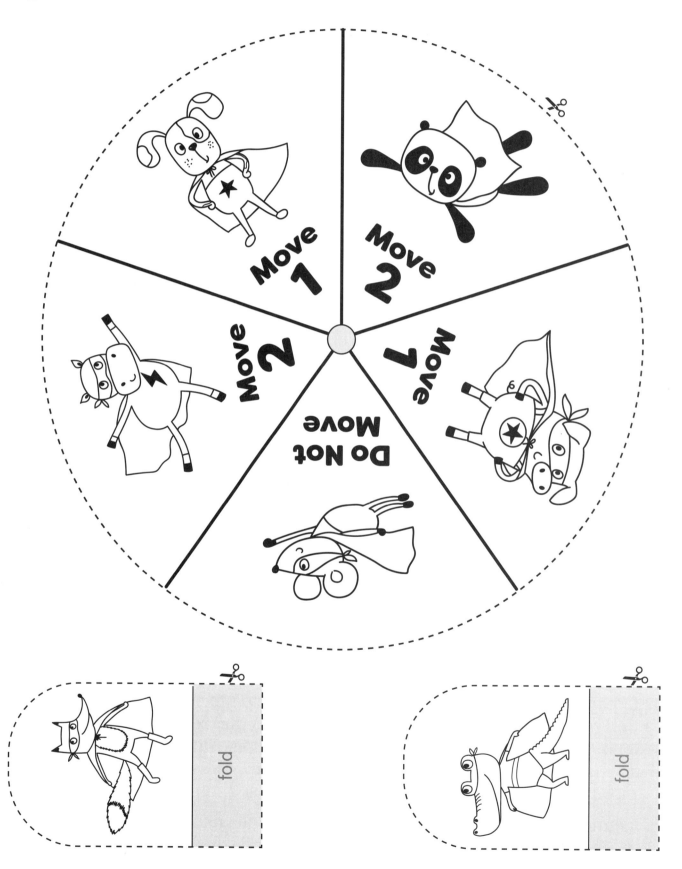

Superhero Cards

protect

suit

mask

cape

smart

strong

brave

power

super

hero

Game Board

ZAP!

START

YAY!

END

Spelling Games and Activities • EMC 8272 • © Evan-Moor Corporation

Extra Practice Worksheets

This section provides an additional 295 words to give students even more practice with spelling patterns and word study! The activity pages can be used independently or to enhance *Building Spelling Skills* weekly lessons.

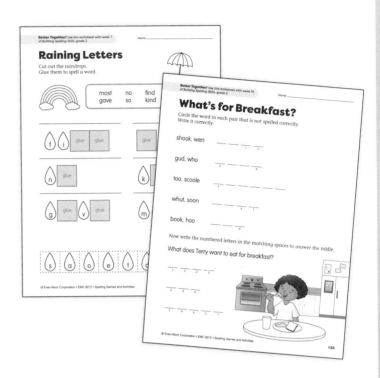

Better Together!

The worksheets in this section correspond to each week in *Building Spelling Skills*, grade 2.

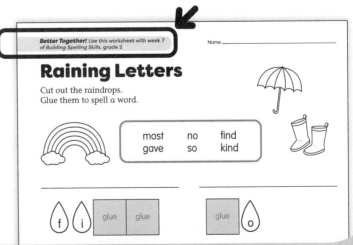

Name _____

Missing Pearl

Write the missing letter to finish the word.
Then cut and glue the pearl with the letter you wrote.

but	get	had	red	on

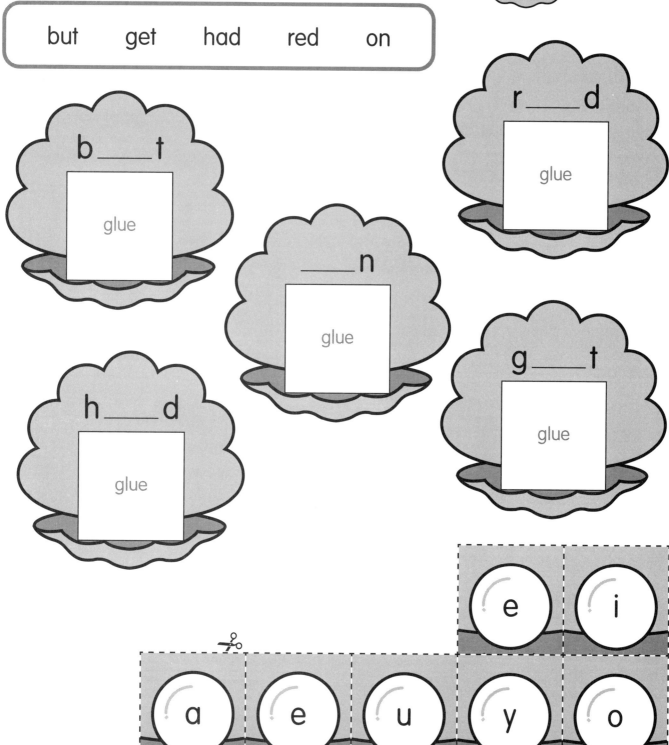

b___t
glue

r___d
glue

___n
glue

h___d
glue

g___t
glue

e   i

a   e   u   y   o

Name _____

Same Shells

Look at the first shell in each row. Color the shell that looks the same.
Then color the circle next to the vowel sound that both words have.

on	hat	hot	net	○ short **a** sound ○ short **o** sound
get	red	dot	rip	○ short **e** sound ○ short **o** sound
did	set	pan	in	○ short **i** sound ○ short **e** sound
hot	can	not	bet	○ short **a** sound ○ short **o** sound
had	pen	but	at	○ short **e** sound ○ short **a** sound

Name _____

Secret Words

The secret words are written in code! Match each shape in the code to a letter. Write the letters to spell each word.

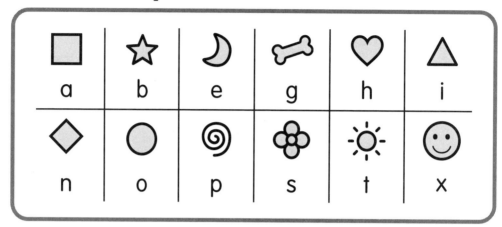

_____ _____ _____   _____ _____ _____

_____ _____ _____   _____ _____ _____

_____ _____ _____   _____ _____

Spell a Meal

Look at the word below the picture.
Circle the foods with the letters to spell the word.

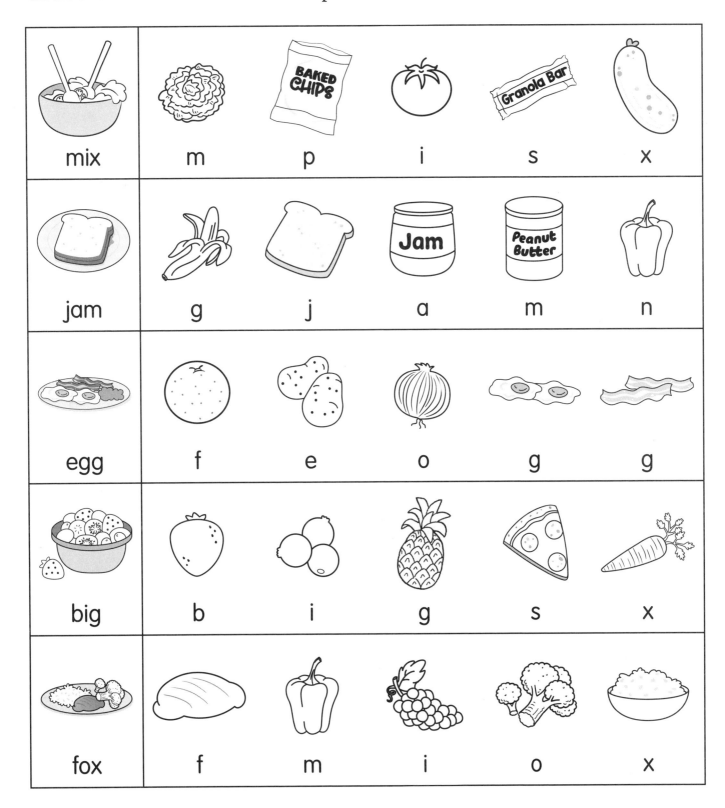

mix	m	p	i	s	x
jam	g	j	a	m	n
egg	f	e	o	g	g
big	b	i	g	s	x
fox	f	m	i	o	x

Name _____

To the Island

Help the ship sail to the island. Write letters to spell a word.
Then connect the circles to spell the word and reach the island.

call   hand   his   land

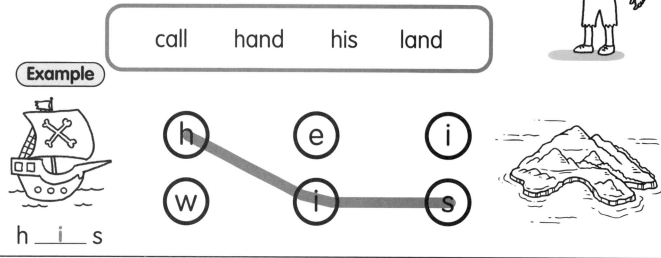

Example

h __i__ s

la __ __ __ __ __

c __ __ __ __ l

ha __ __ __ __ __

Name _____

Treasure Chests

Unscramble the letters to spell a word. Write the word.
Then draw a line to match the words and give the child some treasure.

   na   _____

   his

   lalms   _____

   and

   sih   _____

   small

   dna   _____

   can

   cna   _____

   an

Bus Ride

Help the bus get to school.
Follow the words that have a short vowel sound.

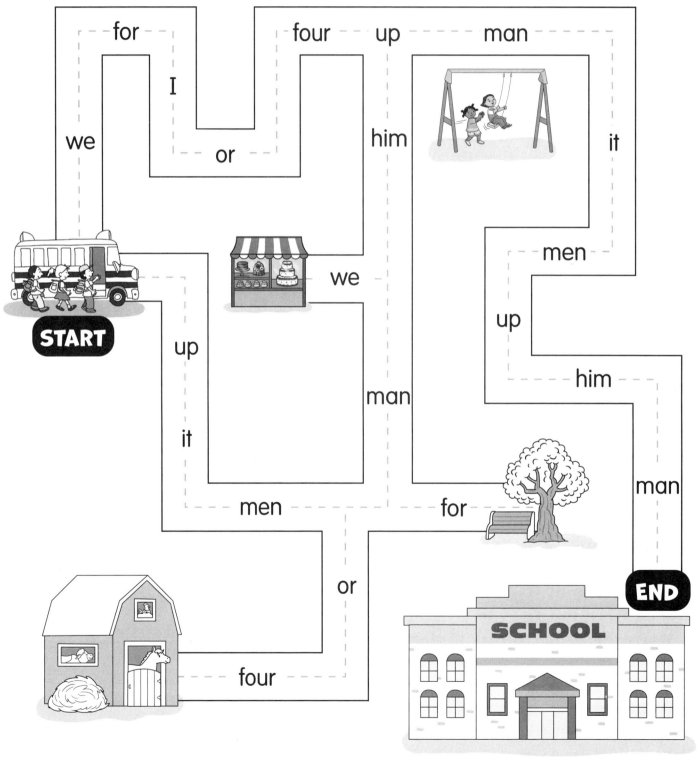

for

four   up   man

I

or

we

him

it

we

men

man

up

up

it

him

men   for

man

or

four

START

END

SCHOOL

Name _____

My Backpack

Write the missing letters to finish spelling each word.
Then draw a line to put the items in the correct backpack.

| for   four   him   man   or   we |

 m _____ _____

words with **r** after
a vowel

 f ____r

 w _____

words with a short
vowel sound

 fo _____ _____

 h ____m

words with a long
vowel sound

 o _____

Hopscotch

Vernon is playing word hopscotch. He can hop only onto the spaces with correctly spelled words. Circle each word that Vernon lands on.

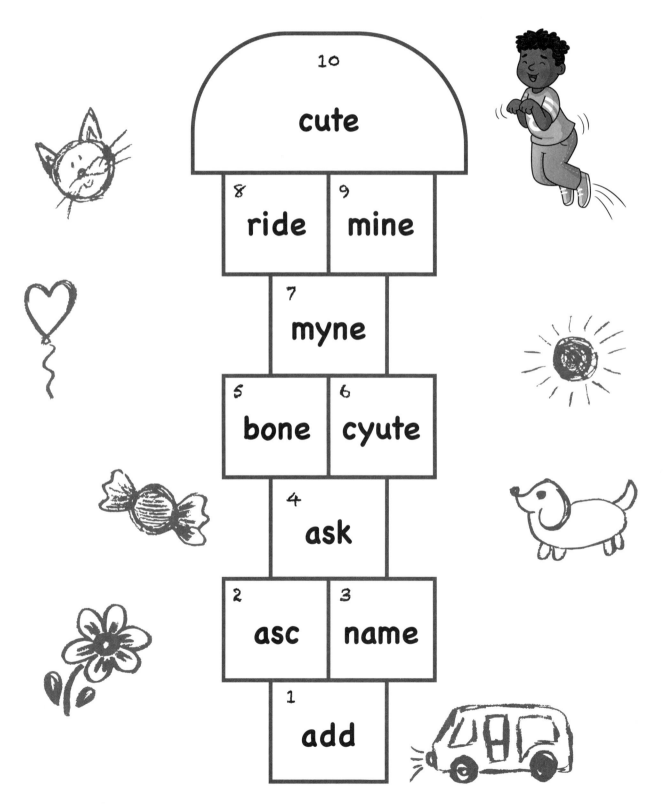

10 cute

8 ride   9 mine

7 myne

5 bone   6 cyute

4 ask

2 asc   3 name

1 add

Name _____

Word Race

Help each runner finish the race.
Color the squares to spell a word.

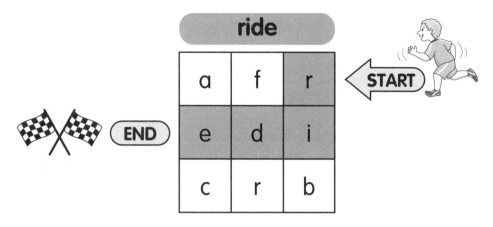

ride

a	f	r
e	d	i
c	r	b

START

END

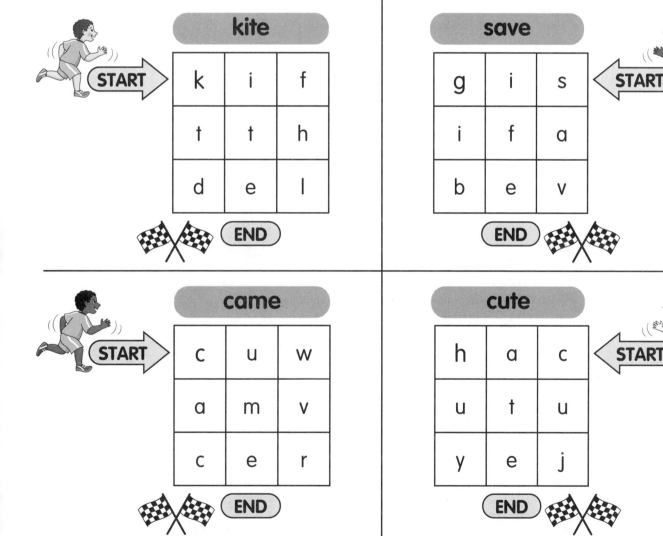

kite

START

k	i	f
t	t	h
d	e	l

END

save

START

g	i	s
i	f	a
b	e	v

END

came

START

c	u	w
a	m	v
c	e	r

END

cute

START

h	a	c
u	t	u
y	e	j

END

Name _____

Day Is Done

The animals have been out all day.
Cut out the animals and glue them in the correct barn.

| words with a **short vowel sound** | words with a **long vowel sound** |

glue

glue

glue

glue

glue

got

be

see

sheep

shop

Name _____

Take a Ride

Circle the word in each pair that is not spelled correctly.
Write it correctly.

shee, see   ___ ___ ___
                              4

be, qween   ___ ___ ___ ___ ___
                                   2

shop, grene   ___ ___ ___ ___ ___
                          1

sheepe, bee   ___ ___ ___ ___ ___
                                        5

got, hee   ___ ___
                        3

Now write the numbered letters in the matching spaces to answer the riddle.
Then color the picture.

What does Femi want to ride in?

a ___ ___ d   j ___ ___ ___
    1   2   3   4   5

Name _____

Write It and Find It

Unscramble the letters to spell a word. Write the word.
Then find and color the picture with the correct spelling of each word.

> do   doing   find   go   going

og _____

od _____

ifdn _____

gongi _____

onigd _____

fynd

doing

dooh

go

do

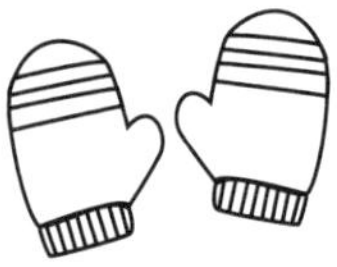

goh

dooing

going

find

goeng

Name _____

Raining Letters

Cut out the raindrops.
Glue them to spell a word.

most	no	find
gave	so	kind

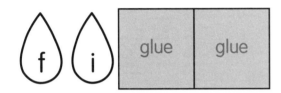

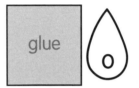

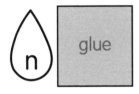

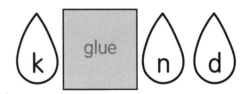

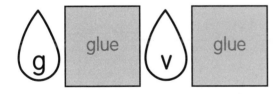

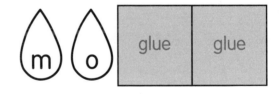

s   a   o   e   t   d   i   s   n

Name _____

How Much?

How much does each shirt cost?
Look at the word on the shirt.
Look at the price for each letter.
Add the letter prices together.
Write the total price of the shirt.

a = $1	d = $2	e = $3
h = $4	m = $5	s = $6
t = $7	w = $8	y = $9

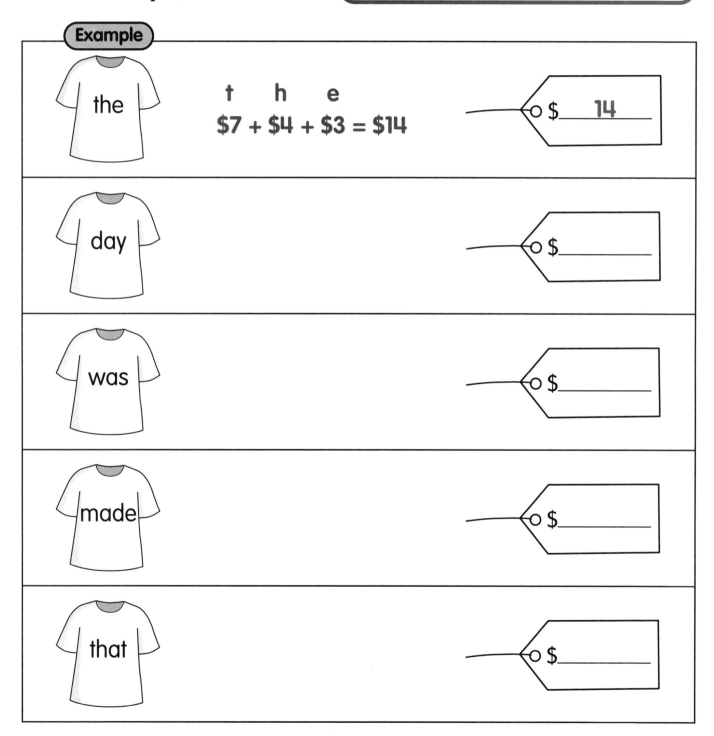

Example

the

t   h   e
$7 + $4 + $3 = $14 $ ___14___

day $ _____

was $ _____

made $ _____

that $ _____

Name _____

Under the Sea

Color the picture.

blue	yellow	orange
starts with **th**	has a **long a** sound	ends in **f**

Name _____

Soccer Puzzle

Cut out the puzzle pieces on page 109.
Glue them below to spell words and make a picture.

glue	glue	glue	glue
glue	glue	glue	glue
glue	glue	glue	glue
glue	glue	glue	glue
glue	glue	glue	glue

Soccer Puzzle, *continued*

Name _____

Rhyme Time

Read the word.
Then write a word or words from the box that rhyme.

help	here	make	nice
place	to	two	want

cake   _____

rice   _____

kelp   _____

moo   _____   _____

space   _____

Which words from the box have a **long u** sound?

_____   _____

Making Words

Cut out the puzzle pieces. Glue them to spell a word.

here   into   making   want

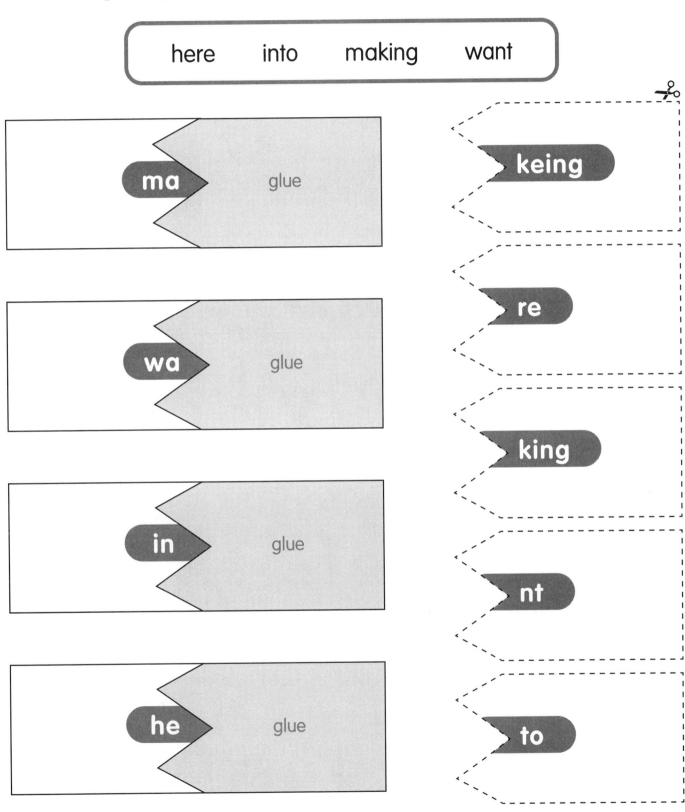

ma   glue

wa   glue

in   glue

he   glue

keing

re

king

nt

to

Name _____

Birthday Gifts

Write the missing letter or letters to finish the word.
Then cut and glue the box with the letters you wrote.

| bath   black   fast   must   send |

se _____ _____

glue

fa _____ _____

m _____ st

bla _____ _____

ba _____ _____

| nd | th | o | u | st | cc | ck |

Same Hats

Look at the first hat in each row. Color the hat that looks the same.
Then color the circle that tells what both words have in common.

Example				
end	ten	ear	send	● **nd** ending ○ **long e** sound
pick	black	pin	kite	○ **long i** sound ○ **ck** ending
bath	bear	both	lap	○ **th** ending ○ **short a** sound
just	jump	men	must	○ **st** ending ○ **long u** sound
fast	but	last	at	○ **long a** sound ○ **st** ending

Name _____

Secret Sentence

The secret words are written in code! Match each shape in the code to
a letter. Write the letters to spell each word and finish the sentence.

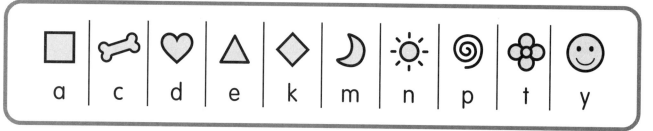

_____ _____   _____ u _____ _____ _____

_____ i _____ _____ , _____

_____ _____ _____ _____   the

_____ _____ _____ _____ _____ .

Name _____

Fruit Bowl

Look at the word below the bowl.
Circle the fruits with the letters to spell the word.

went	w	a	e	n	t
like	j	l	i	k	e
time	t	i	n	m	e
by	b	k	y	c	g
sent	s	e	n	s	t

Name _____

Game Time

Help Nila get to the basketball game.
Follow the words that have only one syllable.

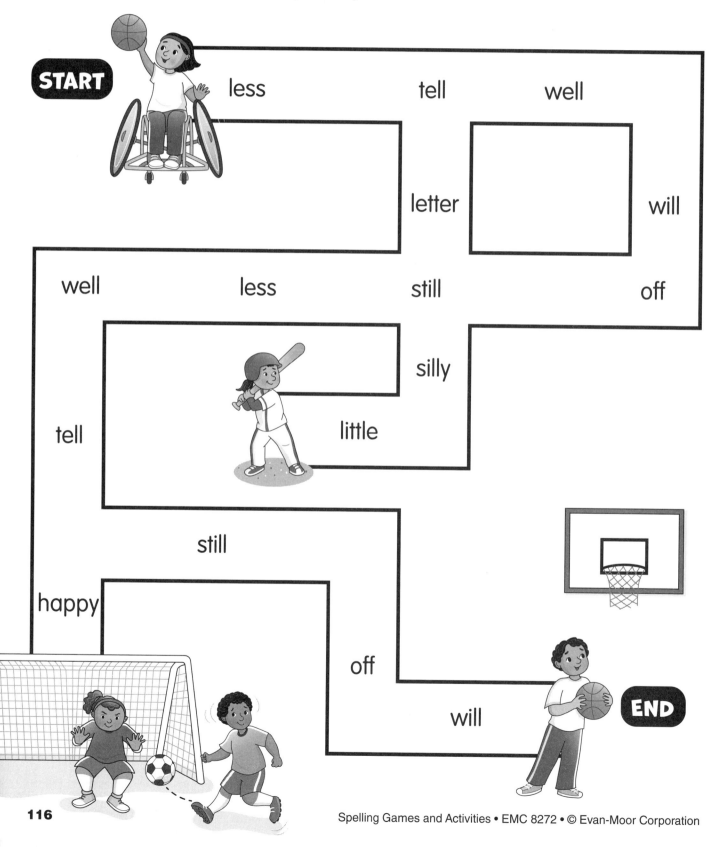

less   tell   well

letter   will

well   less   still   off

silly

tell   little

still

happy   off

will

Name _____

Shoot and Score

Write the missing letters to finish spelling each word.
Then draw a line to shoot the ball into the correct basket.

| happy | letter | little | off | silly | well |

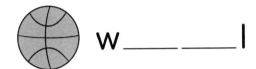 w _____ l

 lit _____ e

 ha _____ y

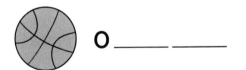 o _____

 lett _____

 si _____ y

words with one syllable

words with two syllables

Name _____

Pick Up the Child

Help the boat sail to the child. Write letters to spell a word.
Then connect the circles to spell the word and reach the child.

boat   coat   fawn   long

Example

bo __a__ __t__

lo _____ _____

f_____ _____n

c_____ _____t

Name _____

Floaties

Unscramble the letters to spell a word. Write the word.
Then draw a line to match the words and give the child a floatie.

 ftalo _____

paw

 wpa _____

float

 lebngo _____

wall

 lawl _____

along

 agnol _____

belong

Name _____

Hopscotch

Bernice is playing word hopscotch. She can hop only onto the spaces with correctly spelled words. Circle each word that Bernice lands on.

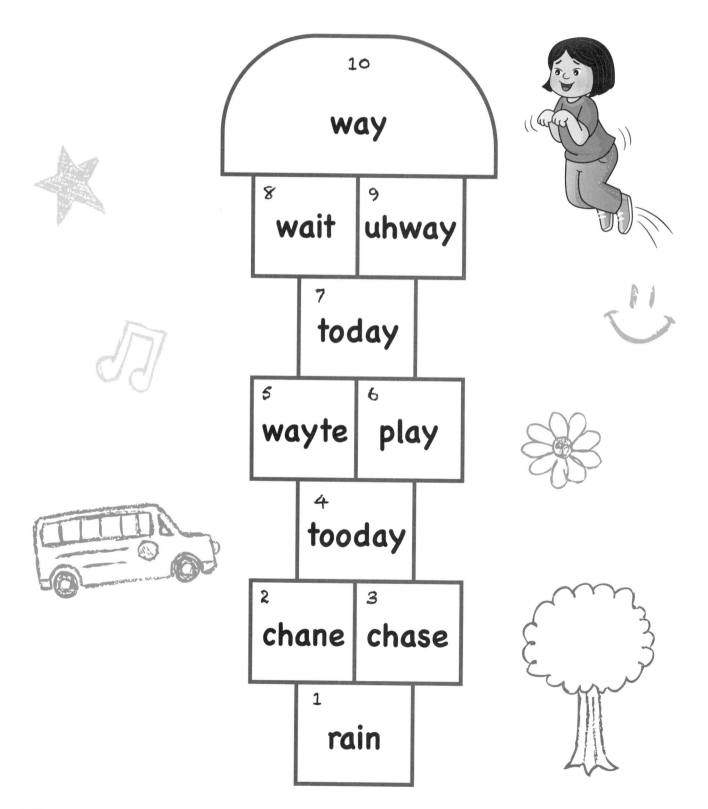

Name _____

Walk Home

Help the children get home. Color the squares to spell a word.

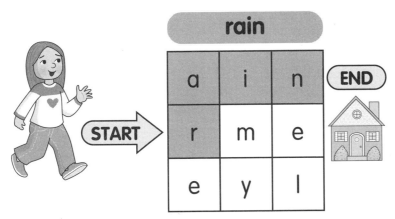

rain

a	i	n
r	m	e
e	y	l

START → ← END

chain

c	h	a
k	y	i
w	g	n

START → END

away

k	h	a
u	e	w
i	y	a

← START END

paint

p	u	a	g
a	i	u	b
y	n	t	i

START → END

played

h	g	l	p
e	y	a	c
d	r	v	i

← START END

Name _____

Toy Cleanup

Help put the toys away.
Cut out the toys and glue them in the correct toy box.

glue

glue   glue

glue

glue   glue

vowel sounds
like **took**

vowel sounds
like **too**

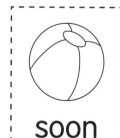 soon  book 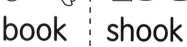 shook  who  school  good

Name _____

What's for Breakfast?

Circle the word in each pair that is not spelled correctly.
Write it correctly.

shook, wen   ___ ___ ___ ___
                         1   5

gud, who   ___ ___ ___ ___
                      2   6

too, scoole   ___ ___ ___ ___ ___ ___
                      3

whut, soon   ___ ___ ___ ___
                            4   7

book, hoo   ___ ___ ___
                            8

Now write the numbered letters in the matching spaces to answer the riddle.

What does Terry want to eat for breakfast?

___ ___ ___ ___
 1   2   2   3

___ ___ ___
 4   5   6

___ ___ ___ ___ ___
 7   8   4   3   7

Name _____

Scrambled Planets

Unscramble the letters to spell a word. Write the word.
Then color each planet that has a word that you wrote.

| house | now | out | shout | show |

whso _____   hueos _____

tuo _____   onw _____

tuohs _____

showt

naw

now

owt

shoaw

shout

howse

show

house

out

Name _____

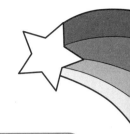

Written in the Stars

Cut out the stars. Glue them to spell a word.

about	down	house	how	our	slow

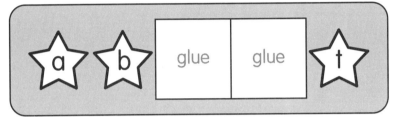

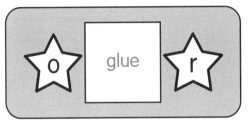

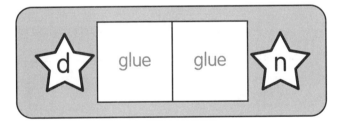

Name _____

Hats for Sale

How much does each hat cost?
Look at the word next to the hat. Look at the price for each letter.
Add the letter prices together. Write the total price of the hat.

a = $1	c = $2	d = $3	e = $4	h = $5
n = $6	r = $7	t = $9	u = $10	

Example

are

a   r   e
$1 + $7 + $4 = $12

$ ___12___

---

her

$ _____

---

card

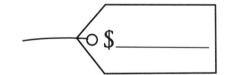

$ _____

---

turn

$ _____

---

hurt

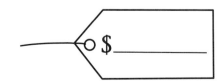

$ _____

Spelling Games and Activities • EMC 8272 • © Evan-Moor Corporation

Garden Vegetable

Color the picture.

brown
words with **ar**

green
words with **er**

orange
words with **ir**

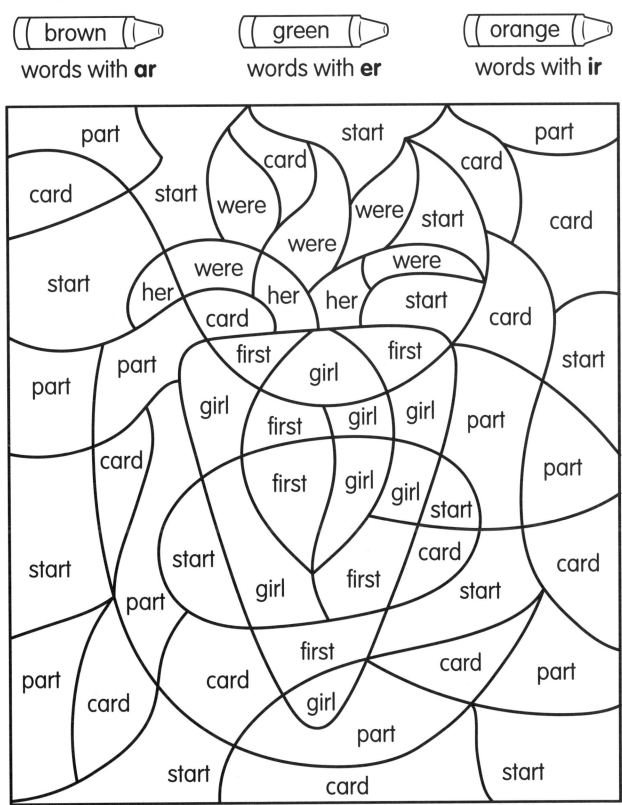

Name _____

Rhyme Time

Read the word.
Then write a word or words from the box that rhyme.

| flew | more | new | stand |
| star | sting | stone | |

 store _____

 ring _____

 bone _____

 hand _____

 jar _____

 blew _____ _____

Which words from the box have a short vowel sound?

_____ _____

Name _____

Making Words

Cut out the puzzle pieces. Glue them to spell a word.

| more   new   ring   star |

st   glue

mo   glue

n   glue

ri   glue

ng

arr

ew

re

ar

Name _____

Catch It

Write the missing letters to finish the word.
Then cut and glue the baseball with the letters you wrote.

friend   from   love   such   told

s ____ ch

glue

frie ____

glue

l ____ ve

glue

____ om

glue

to ____

glue

✂

ld   ch   o   u   fr   nd   ve

Same Uniform

Look at the first shirt in each row. Color the shirt that looks the same.
Then color the circle that tells what both words have in common.

Example				
have	ten	gave	ear	● **ve** ending ○ **long e** sound
friend	from	fan	lake	○ **fr** beginning ○ **nd** ending
old	our	pile	told	○ **long o** sound ○ **short o** sound
live	frog	blank	give	○ **long i** sound ○ **silent e** ending
much	hip	such	bat	○ **long u** sound ○ **ch** ending

Name _____

Feeding Time Puzzle

Cut out the puzzle pieces on page 133.
Glue them below to spell words and make a picture.

glue	glue	glue	glue
glue	glue	glue	glue
glue	glue	glue	glue
glue	glue	glue	glue
glue	glue	glue	glue

Feeding Time Puzzle, *continued*

Grandmother's House

Help Rosie get to her grandmother's house.
Follow the words that end in **er**.

START

sister   brother   mother

boil

other

boy

oil   father

soil   toy   mother

other

father

oil   toy   soil

boil   sister

oil   boy   brother   **END**

Name _____

Bear Family

Write the missing letters to finish spelling each word.
Then draw a line to match the cub with its parent.

> boil   father   other   sister   soil   toy

 fath____ ____

 s____ ____l

 o____ ____er

 b____ ____l

 t____ ____

 sist____ ____

ends in **er**

has the diphthong **oi** or **oy**

Name _____

Beehive

Help the bee fly to the hive. Write letters to spell a word.
Then connect the circles to spell the word and reach the hive.

bank   then   this   with

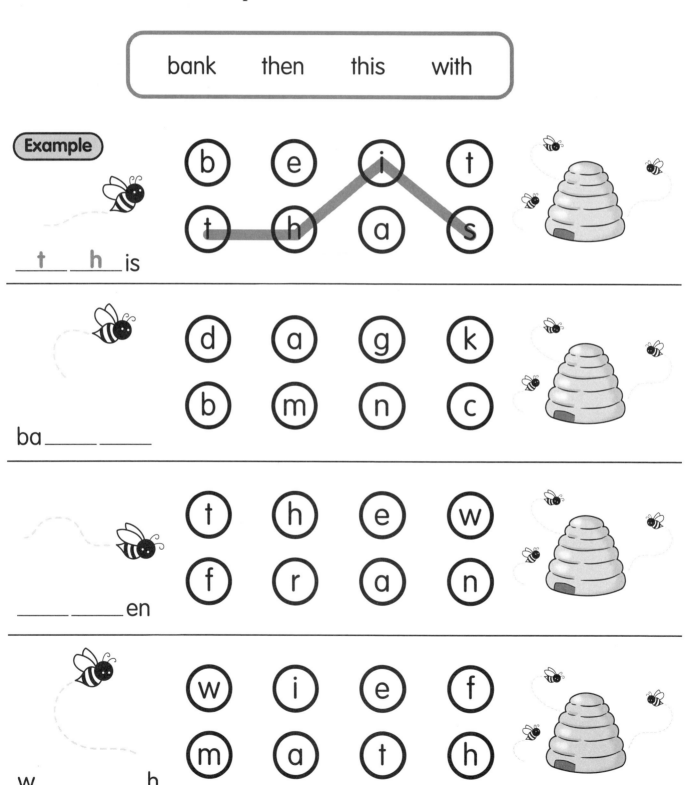

Example

____t____ ____h____ is

ba _____ _____

_____ _____ en

w _____ _____ h

Name _____

Hungry Bugs

Unscramble the letters to spell a word. Write the word.
Then draw a line to match the words and give each bug a flower.

 nkhat   _____

 thank

 sngi   _____

 thing

 seeth   _____

 sing

 hisw   _____

 wish

 ghitn   _____

 these

Name _____

Secret Words

The secret words are written in code! Match each shape in the code to a letter. Write the letters to spell each word.

⬜	☆	🦴	♡	△	◇
a	d	e	g	i	n
🌙	☼	@	✿	☺	
r	s	t	u	y	

_____ _____ _____

_____ _____ _____ _____ _____

_____ _____ _____ _____ _____

_____ _____ _____ _____

_____ _____ _____ _____ _____ _____

Name _____

Candy Jar

Look at the word below the jar.
Circle the candy with the letters to spell the word.

fly	j	f	l	i	y
eat	e	d	a	t	n
mean	m	e	a	c	n
each	e	a	g	c	h
why	w	a	h	u	y

Name _____

Hopscotch

Joy is playing word hopscotch. She can hop only onto the spaces with correctly spelled words. Circle each word that Joy lands on.

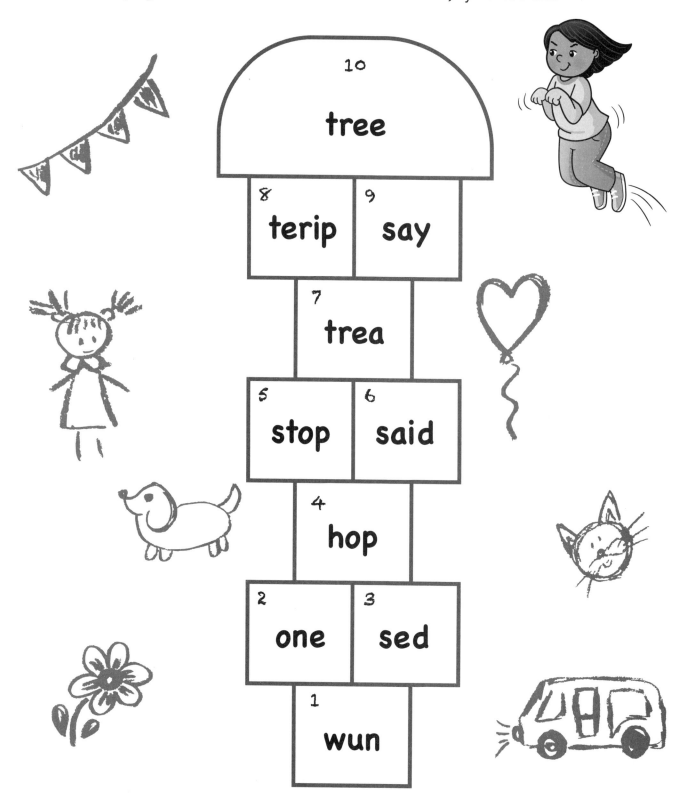

Name _____

Swim Home

Help the fish reach the reef. Color the squares to spell a word.

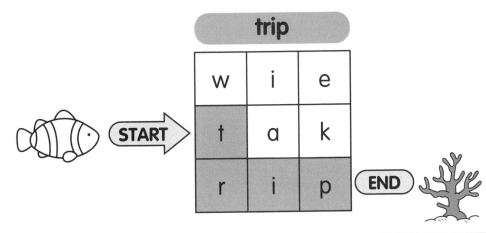

trip

w	i	e
t	a	k
r	**i**	**p**

START → | END

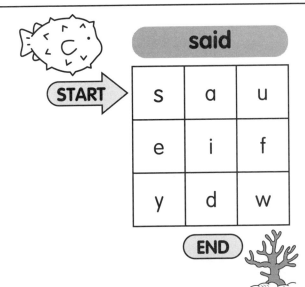

said

s	a	u
e	i	f
y	d	w

START → | END

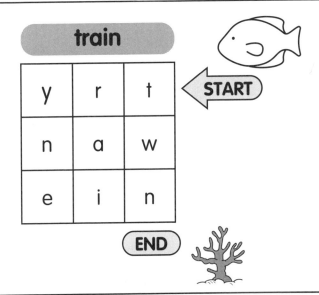

train

y	r	t
n	a	w
e	i	n

← START | END

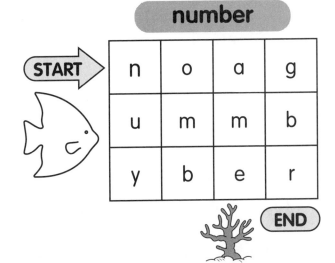

number

n	o	a	g
u	m	m	b
y	b	e	r

START → | END

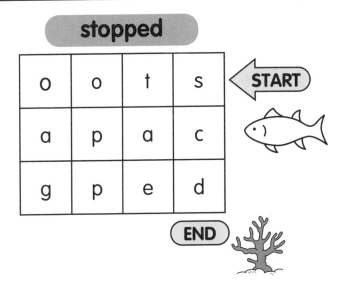

stopped

o	o	t	s
a	p	a	c
g	p	e	d

← START | END

Name _____

Doghouse

Oh no! The dogs got out of the fence!
Cut out the dogs and glue them in the correct house.

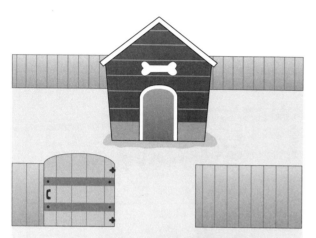

words with a **double letter**

glue

glue

glue

words that end in **ck**

glue

glue

glue

stick

quick

cook

root

back

look

Name _____

Visit the Animals

Circle the word in each pair that is not spelled correctly.
Write it correctly.

zue, stick   ___ ___ ___
                   1

lookt, root   ___ ___ ___ ___ ___ ___
                                  2

bak, look   ___ ___ ___ ___
                   3

quick, tric   ___ ___ ___ ___ ___
                       4

cook, pak   ___ ___ ___ ___
                       5

Now write the numbered letters in the matching spaces to answer the riddle.

What animal at the zoo is black with white stripes?

a   ___ ___ ___ ___ ___
    1   2   3   4   5

Name _____

Gift Cost

How much does each gift cost?
Look at the word on the gift. Look at the price for each letter.
Add the letter prices together. Write the total price of the gift.

a = $1	b = $2	c = $3	e = $4	f = $5	g = $6
i = $7	k = $8	m = $9	n = $10	r = $11	t = $12

Example

   t   a   g
$12 + $1 + $6 = $19

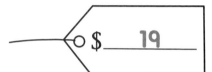 $ _____19_____

 gift

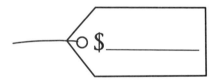 $ _____

 cake

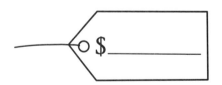 $ _____

 game

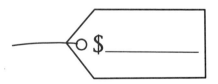 $ _____

 bring

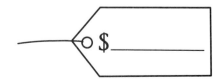 $ _____

Birthday Cake

Color the picture.

pink
starts with **ch**

brown
starts with
pr or **br**

yellow
ends with **y**

blue
ends with
silent **e**

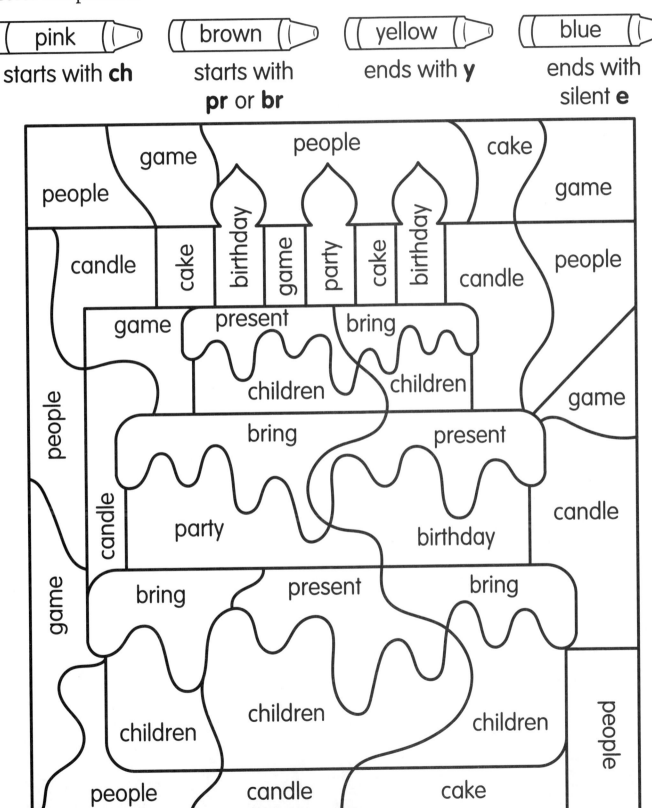

Name _____

Rhyme Time

Read the word.
Then write a word or words from the box that rhyme.

| brown | found | push | put | round | would |

could   _____

frown   _____

bush   _____

around   _____ _____

foot   _____

Which rhyming words have different vowels?

_____ _____

Name _____

Making Words

Cut out the puzzle pieces. Glue them to spell a word.

around   could   pull   something

pu | glue

und

aro | glue

thing

d

cou | glue

ld

some | glue

ll

Name _____

Monkey Puzzle

Cut out the puzzle pieces on page 149.
Glue them below to spell words and make a picture.

glue	glue	glue	glue
glue	glue	glue	glue
glue	glue	glue	glue
glue	glue	glue	glue
glue	glue	glue	glue

Monkey Puzzle, *continued*

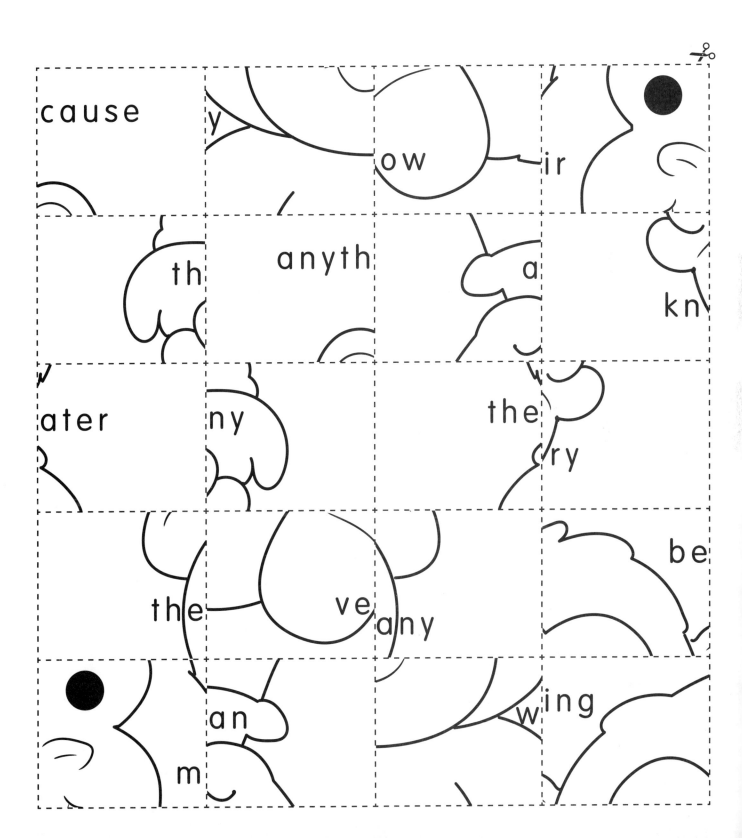

Name _____

Write It and Find It

Unscramble the letters to spell a word. Write the word.
Then circle the picture with the correct spelling of each word.

after	inside	over	under	where

derun _____   vreo _____

seindi _____   ehwre _____

tafer _____

enside

over

under

ovor

undar

after

where

aftat

inside

wheer

Name _____

Frog Pond

Cut out the raindrops.
Glue them to spell a word.

again	before	outside
there	which	

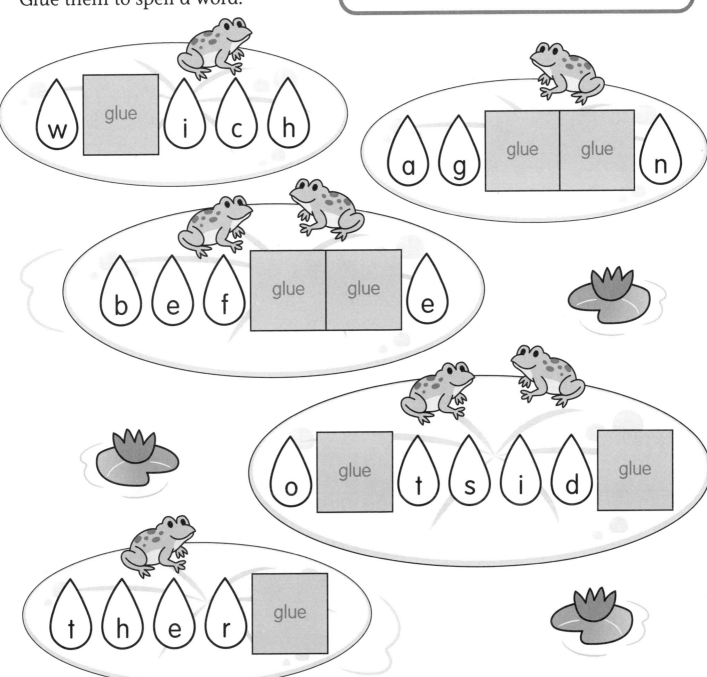

Spelling Strategies

How to Spell Hard Words

There are so many words! It is hard to remember how to spell them all. You need a plan when you are writing. Use these ways to try to spell words that you don't know.

	Say the word. Listen to the sounds. Count the syllables. (Ask yourself) What do I hear? What do I know?
i before e except after c	**Think about rules** using the sounds you heard. (Ask yourself) Is there a rule or pattern I can follow?
-ice family mice nice rice price slice spice twice	**Think about words** that you can spell. (Ask yourself) Does it rhyme with another word? Is it part of a word family?
day|dream|ing	**Break up the word into parts.** Divide compound words. Divide into syllables. Divide after a prefix. Divide before an ending. (Ask yourself) How can I break it into small parts?
success sŭk sĕs´ **to do well**	**Try to spell the word.** You can try different ways. (Ask yourself) Does it look right? Is it in the dictionary?

Spelling Strategies

Spell Vowel Sounds

Every word has a vowel sound. There are different kinds of vowel sounds. Look at the chart to find the kind you hear in a word.

I hear a short vowel sound.

Write the letter you hear:

th**a**n, h**e**lp, l**i**st, fr**o**g, m**u**ch, tr**y**

Or try a vowel pair:

h**ea**d, fri**e**nd, s**aw**

I hear a long vowel sound.

Write the letter you hear and a silent **e** after the consonant:

s**a**v**e**, th**e**s**e**, r**i**d**e**, h**o**s**e**, c**u**b**e**

Or try a vowel pair:

l**ai**d, tod**ay**, bab**ie**s, b**ea**n, s**ee**n, s**oa**p, l**ow**, y**ou**, r**oo**m

I hear a schwa sound.

A vowel can have a schwa sound:

about, happ**e**n, penc**i**l, bott**o**m, **u**pon

Make a guess. Write the word:
- See if it looks right.
- Check the dictionary.
- Make up a memory clue.

I hear something else.

R-controlled vowels are not short or long. Write the vowel that sounds closest.

h**a**rd, h**e**r, b**i**rd, h**o**rse, t**u**rn

Diphthongs are letter pairs that make two sounds:

f**oi**l, j**oy**, h**ou**se, t**ow**n

Spelling Strategies

Spell Consonant Sounds

Some consonants have two sounds. Look at the chart.
Find the sound you hear in a word.

J I hear a **j** sound.

Write a **j** most of the time:

> en**j**oy, **j**ury

Write a **g** before an **e** or **i** sound.
Write a **g** if you hear it at the end.

> a**g**e, **gi**ant, chan**g**e

S I hear an **s** sound.

Write an **s** most of the time:

> **s**ave, **s**un, al**s**o, a**s**k, u**s**

Write a **c** before an **e** or **i** sound:

> **ce**nter, re**ci**tal,
> accura**cy**

K I hear a **k** sound.

Write a **c** most of the time:

> **c**arry, **co**me, **cu**te, **cl**ip

Write a **k** before an **e** or **i** sound.
Write a **k** if you hear it at the end.

> **k**eep, **ki**te, li**k**e

F I hear an **f** sound.

Write an **f** or **ph** at the
beginning. Write an **f**, **ff**, or **ph**
in the middle or at the end.

> **f**all, **ph**one, a**f**ter,
> di**ff**erent, al**ph**abet,
> **if**, o**ff**, gra**ph**

? I hear **something else.**

Some **pairs** have their own sound:

> ea**ch**, **sh**ut, nor**th**, **wh**y

? What am I **not hearing**?

Some words have **silent letters**:

> si**g**n, wa**l**k, lis**t**en, **k**now

Spelling Strategies

Break Down Words

Break long words into smaller pieces. They are easier to spell that way.

Divide compound words.

Compound words are made of two shorter words put together.

1. Say the word.

   fishnet

2. Write the two words that are in the compound word.

   fish
   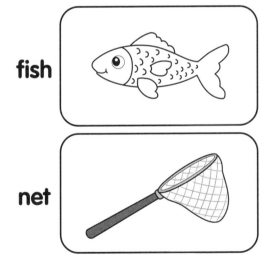

   net

3. Spell the smaller words.

   fishnet

Divide words into syllables.

Syllables are short pieces of a word. Each syllable has a vowel sound. Every time you say a syllable, your chin moves.

1. Say the word.

   strawberry

2. Listen to each syllable. Write the sounds in each one.

   straw – ber – ry

3. Spell the syllables together.

   strawberry

Spelling Strategies
Use Suffixes

You can make more words from words you know. Just add a suffix.

Make words for more than one thing.

Most nouns: add **s**	Nouns ending in **s**, **ss**, **sh**, or **ch**: add **es**	Nouns ending in **y**: drop the **y**, add **ies**
tree**s**, mat**s**, bed**s**	bus**es**, glass**es**, wish**es**, rich**es**	stor**ies**

Make describing words.

Most words: add **er**, **est**, **ly**, **ful**, **ness**, **less**	Words ending in **y**: change **y** to **i** and add the suffix
hard**er**, high**est**, friend**ly**, care**ful**, great**ness**, fear**less**	happ**ier**, happ**iest**, happ**ily**, happ**iness**

Change action words.

Most verbs: add **ed** or **ing**	Verbs ending in **e**: drop the **e** and add **ed** or **ing**	Verbs ending in **y**: change **y** to **i** and add **ed**
wash**ed**, go**ing**	lik**ed**, clos**ing**	stud**ied**, cr**ied**

Spelling Games and Activities • EMC 8272 • © Evan-Moor Corporation

Spelling Strategies
Use a Dictionary

A dictionary tells about words. It helps you spell them and say them. It tells you what they mean.

How to find a word

"I don't know how to spell it. How can I look it up?"

Guess at the spelling. Try **howce.** Is it in the dictionary?
If not, try **houce**.
Is it in the dictionary?
If not, try **house**.
Keep trying until you find it.

How to say a word

"I have seen that word. But what does it sound like?"

Find the word in the dictionary. Look at the symbols. They tell you short and long vowels and consonant sounds.

It also shows the syllables.
enough (ē nŭf´)

How to learn a word's meanings

"I can read the word. But what does it mean?"

Find the word in the dictionary. You will see what it means. Some words mean more than one thing.

kind (kīnd)

1. nice 2. a type or group

Spelling Strategies

Make Memory Clues

Some words don't follow rules. You can make up your own memory clues to help you remember them!

Make a jump-rope rhyme.

F-R-I-E-N-D.
Be the best friend you can be!

Make a hand-clapping rhyme.

H-O-L-I-D-A-Y.
Let's get together and bake a pie.

Make a word hopscotch.

Say the letter or letters as you land on them.

GREAT SPELLER!

I completed this book!

Name _____

Answer Key

Page 12

Page 13

Page 14

Page 16
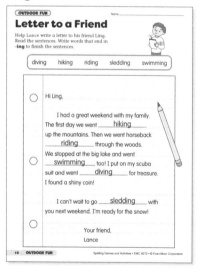

Page 17
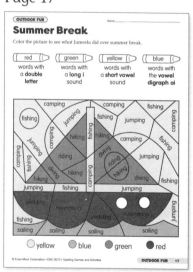

Page 18

Page 22

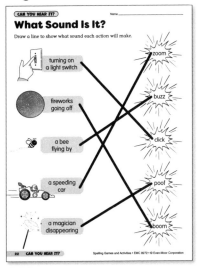

Page 23

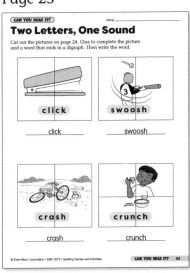

Page 25

Page 26

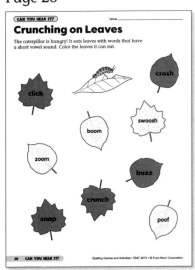

Page 27

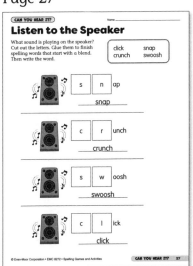

Page 32

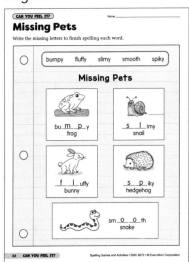

Page 33

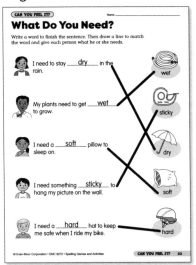

Page 34

Page 36

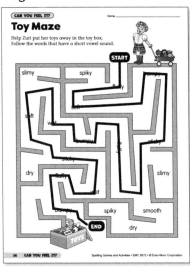

Page 37

Page 42

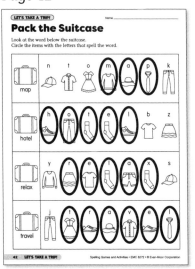

Page 43

Page 45

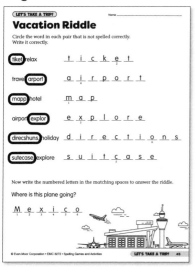

Page 46

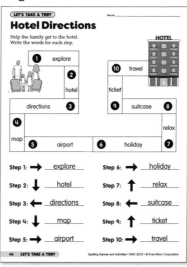

Page 47

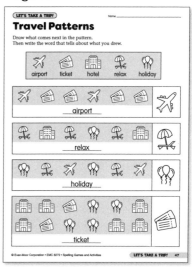

Page 52

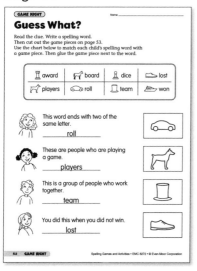

Page 53

Page 54

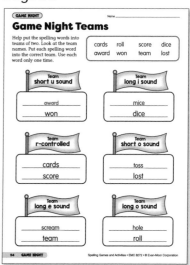

Page 55

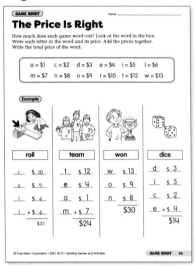

Page 56

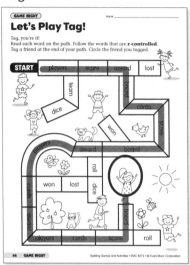

Page 57

Page 62

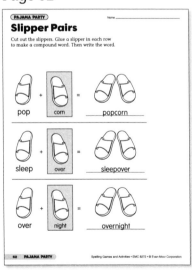

Page 63

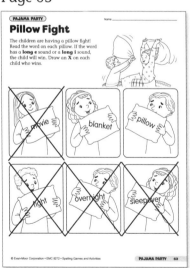

Page 64

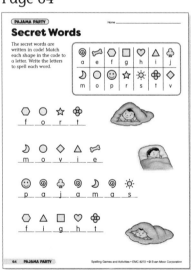

Page 65

Page 66

Page 67

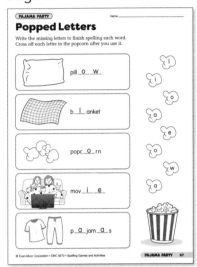

Page 72

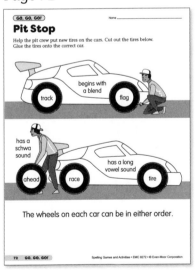

Page 73

Page 74

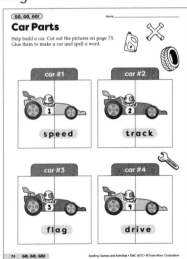

Page 76

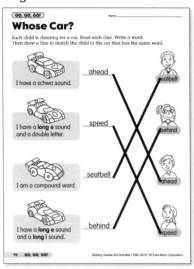

Page 77

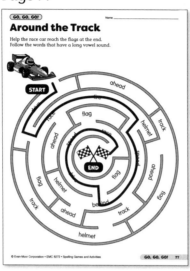

Page 82

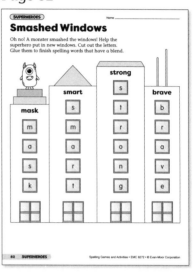

Page 83

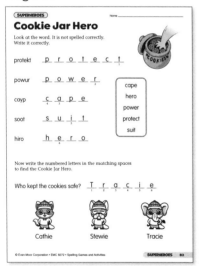

Page 84

Page 85

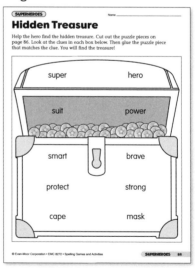

Page 92

Page 93

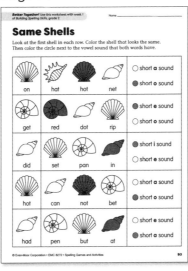

Page 94

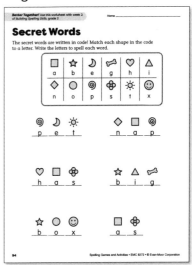

Page 95

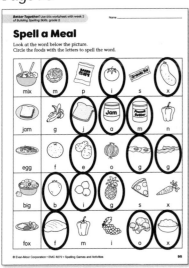

Page 96

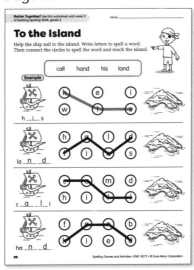

Page 97

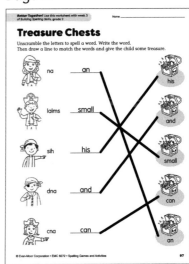

Page 98

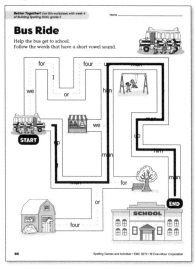

Page 99

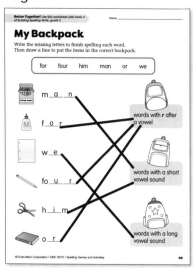

Page 100

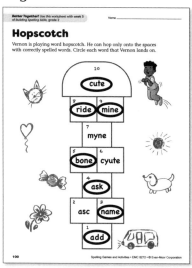

Page 101

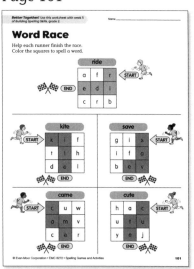

Page 102

Page 103

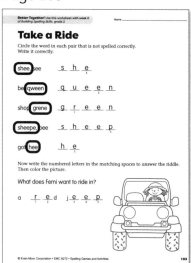

Page 104

Page 105

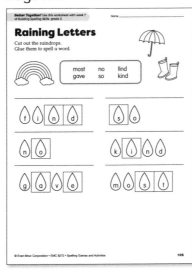

Page 106

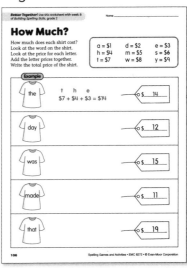

Page 107

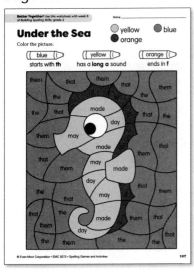

Page 108

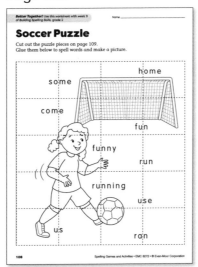

Page 110

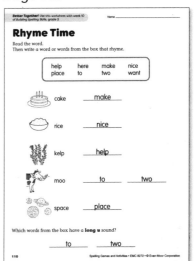

Page 111

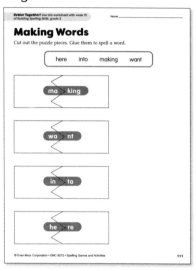

Page 112

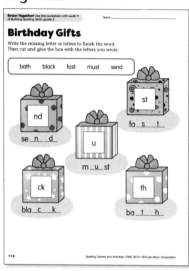

Page 113

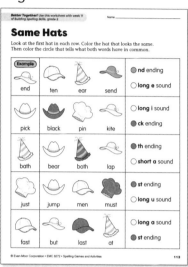

Page 114

Page 115

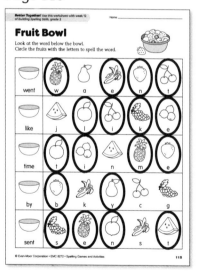

Page 116

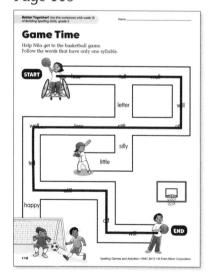

Page 117

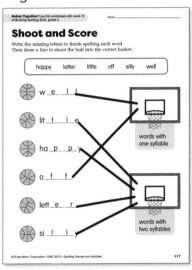

Shoot and Score

Write the missing letters to finish spelling each word.
Then draw a line to shoot the ball into the correct basket.

| happy | letter | little | off | silly | well |

w e l l

lit t l e

ha p p y

o f f

lett e r

si l l y

words with one syllable

words with two syllables

Page 118

Pick Up the Child

Help the boat sail to the child. Write letters to spell a word.
Then connect the circles to spell the word and reach the child.

| boat | coat | fawn | long |

Example

bo a t

lo n g

f a w n

c o a t

Page 119

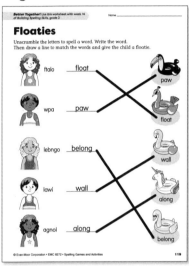

Floaties

Unscramble the letters to spell a word. Write the word.
Then draw a line to match the words and give the child a floatie.

ftalo — float — paw

wpa — paw — float

lebngo — belong — wall

lawi — wall — along

agnol — along — belong

Page 120

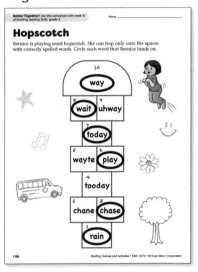

Hopscotch

Bernice is playing word hopscotch. She can hop only onto the spaces
with correctly spelled words. Circle each word that Bernice lands on.

10
8 way 9
wait uhway
7 today
5 6
wayte play
4 tooday
2 3
chane chase
1 rain

Page 121

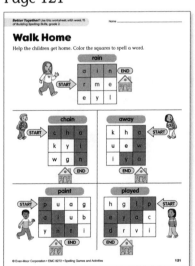

Walk Home

Help the children get home. Color the squares to spell a word.

rain

chain   away

paint   played

Page 122

Toy Cleanup

Help put the toys away.
Cut out the toys and glue them in the correct toy box.

book   soon

shook good   school who

vowel sounds like **took**   vowel sounds like **too**

The words in each box can be in any order.

Page 123

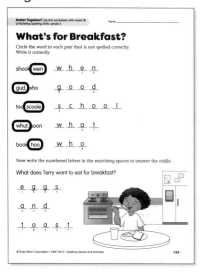

Page 124

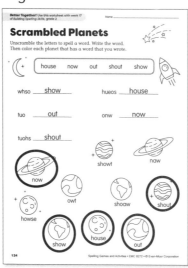

Page 125

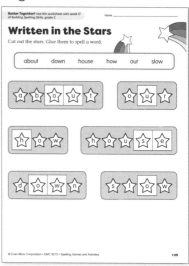

Page 126

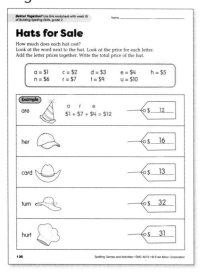

Page 127

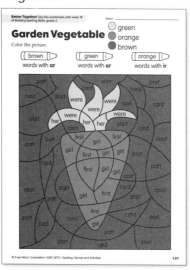

Page 128

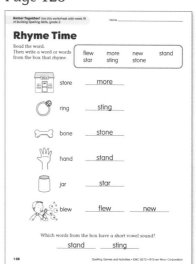

Page 129

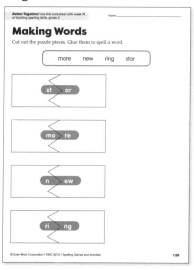

Page 130

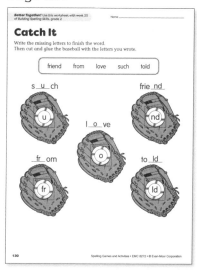

Page 131

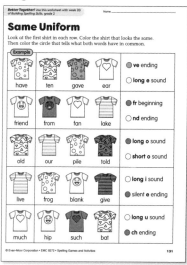

Page 132

Page 134

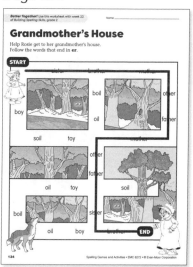

Page 135

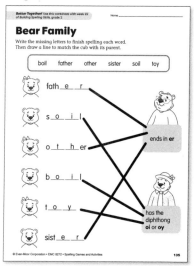

Page 136

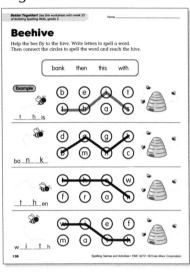

Page 137

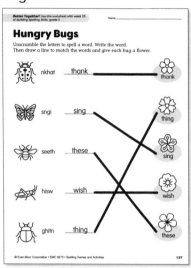

Page 138

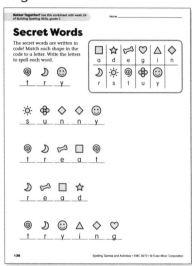

Page 139

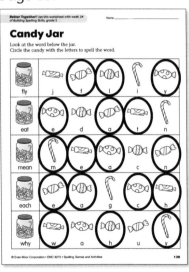

Page 140

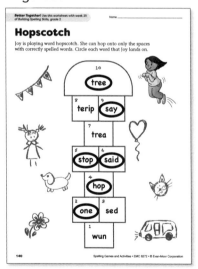

Page 141

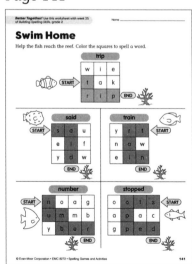

Page 142

Doghouse

Oh no! The dogs got out of the fence!
Cut out the dogs and glue them in the correct house.

words with a **double letter**   words that end in **ck**

cook   stick

root   look   quick   back

The words in each house can be in any order.

Page 143

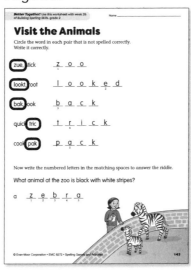

Visit the Animals

Circle the word in each pair that is not spelled correctly.
Write it correctly.

zue, tick   z o o
lookt, root   l o o k e d
bak, look   b a c k
quick tric   t r i c k
cook pak   p a c k

Now write the numbered letters in the matching spaces to answer the riddle.

What animal at the zoo is black with white stripes?

a z e b r a

Page 144

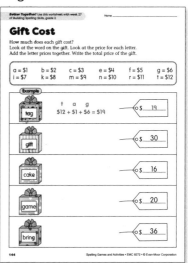

Gift Cost

How much does each gift cost?
Look at the word on the gift. Look at the price for each letter.
Add the letter prices together. Write the total price of the gift.

a = $1	b = $2	c = $3	e = $4	f = $5	g = $6
i = $7	k = $8	m = $9	n = $10	r = $11	t = $12

Example

tag   t a g $12 + $1 + $6 = $19 $ 19

gift $ 30
cake $ 16
game $ 20
bring $ 36

Page 145

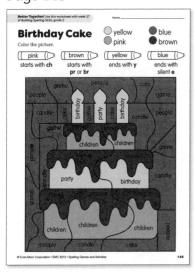

Birthday Cake

Color the picture.

○ yellow   ● blue
○ pink   ● brown

pink — starts with **ch**
brown — starts with **pr or br**
yellow — ends with **y**
blue — ends with silent **e**

Page 146

Rhyme Time

Read the word.
Then write a word or words from the box that rhyme.

brown	found	push	put	round	would

could   would
frown   brown
bush   push
around   found   round
foot   put

Which rhyming words have different vowels?

foot   put

Page 147

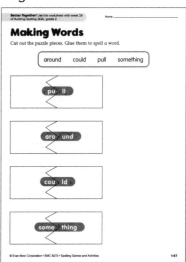

Making Words

Cut out the puzzle pieces. Glue them to spell a word.

around   could   pull   something

pu ll
aro und
cou ld
some thing

Page 148

Monkey Puzzle
Cut out the puzzle pieces on page 149.
Glue them below to spell words and make a picture.

anything   because
their   many
they   water
than   any
know   very

148   Spelling Games and Activities • EMC 8272 • © Evan-Moor Corporation

Page 150

Write It and Find It
Unscramble the letters to spell a word. Write the word.
Then circle the picture with the correct spelling of each word.

| after | inside | over | under | where |

derun ___under___   vreo ___over___

seindi ___inside___   ehwre ___where___

tafer ___after___

150   Spelling Games and Activities • EMC 8272 • © Evan-Moor Corporation

Page 151

Frog Pond
Cut out the raindrops.
Glue them to spell a word.

| again | before | outside |
| there | which | |

w h i c h
a g a i n
b e f o r e
o u t s i d e
t h e r e

© Evan-Moor Corporation • EMC 8272 • Spelling Games and Activities   151